Praise for
Said I Wasn't Gonna Tell Nobody

"James Cone wrote theology in the searing, radiant, liberationist spirit of James Baldwin. His memoir of what set him on fire, how he wrote and taught theology, and mined his inspirations is riveting, stylish, scalding, and luminous." —**Gary Dorrien**, author, *Breaking White Supremacy: Martin Luther King Jr. and the Black Social Gospel*

"This is James Cone's story of how he found his voice and what he used it to say. The result is both eloquent and unflinching in its condemnation of white supremacy. There is redemption in this book, but it is never cheap." —**Tom F. Driver**, Union Theological Seminary

"*¡Alabanza hermano James!* for providing an intimate, intelligent, and insightful testimony to the power of liberation from the underside of a Eurocentric white-supremacist theology. *¡Gracias!* for your faithful witness through word and action." —**Miguel A. De La Torre**, Iliff School of Theology

"James H. Cone provides his personal reflections on what motivated him to depart from his academic training and undertake the novel journey toward becoming the pioneer black theologian. It is a fitting finale to his life and work." —**Peter J. Paris,** Princeton Theological Seminary

"Few have voiced the unbearable sorrow and unbreakable beauty of the African American soul as powerfully as James Cone. This memoir is his 'last will and testament' to those who will continue the struggle for human dignity that he waged so passionately, eloquently, and uncompromisingly." —**Bryan N. Massingale, S.T.D.**, Fordham University

"James Cone has shared his mission to articulate the faith for the oppressed and surface the Gospel for the rest of us. His voice is bold and haunting." —**David O. Woodyard**, Denison University

"*Said I Wasn't Gonna Tell Nobody* is the final masterpiece from the genius architect of Black Liberation theology and the greatest theologian of the twentieth century." —**Anthony G. Reddie**, The University of South Africa and editor, *Black Theology: An International Journal*

Also by James H. Cone

Black Theology and Black Power

The Spirituals and the Blues

God of the Oppressed

My Soul Looks Back

For My People: Black Theology and the Black Church

A Black Theology of Liberation

Speaking the Truth:
Ecumenism, Liberation, and Black Theology

Martin & Malcolm & America: A Dream or a Nightmare

Black Theology: A Documentary History
Volume 1: 1966–1979 (with Gayraud S. Wilmore)

Black Theology: A Documentary History
Volume 2: 1980–1992 (with Gayraud S. Wilmore)

Risks of Faith:
The Emergence of a Black Theology of Liberation, 1968–1998

The Cross and the Lynching Tree

Said I Wasn't Gonna Tell Nobody:
The Making of a Black Theologian

Said I Wasn't Gonna Tell Nobody

Said I Wasn't Gonna Tell Nobody

The Making of a Black Theologian

JAMES H. CONE

ORBIS BOOKS
Maryknoll, New York

ORBIS BOOKS
Maryknoll, New York 10545

Fathers and Brothers
MARYKNOLL

Founded in 1970, Orbis Books endeavors to publish works that enlighten the mind, nourish the spirit, and challenge the conscience. The publishing arm of the Maryknoll Fathers and Brothers, Orbis seeks to explore the global dimensions of the Christian faith and mission, to invite dialogue with diverse cultures and religious traditions, and to serve the cause of reconciliation and peace. The books published reflect the views of their authors and do not represent the official position of the Maryknoll Society. To learn more about Maryknoll and Orbis Books, please visit our website at www.maryknollsociety.org.

Library of Congress Cataloging-in-Publication Data

Names: Cone, James H., author.
Title: Said I wasn't gonna tell nobody : the making of a Black theologian / James H. Cone.
Description: Maryknoll : Orbis Books, 2018. | Includes bibliographical references and index.
Identifiers: LCCN 2018010522 (print) | LCCN 2018026630 (ebook) | ISBN 9781608337682 (e-book) | ISBN 9781626983021 (cloth)
Subjects: LCSH: Cone, James H. | Theologians—United States—Biography. | Black theology—History of doctrines.
Classification: LCC BX4827.C65 (ebook) | LCC BX4827.C65 A3 2018 (print) | DDC 230.092 [B] —dc23
LC record available at https://lccn.loc.gov/2018010522

To the students and faculty of
Union Theological Seminary,
who challenged and inspired me
for nearly a half century.

I Said I Wasn't Gonna Tell Nobody

Chorus
I said I wasn't gonna tell nobody, but I
Couldn't keep it to myself!
Couldn't keep it to myself!
Couldn't keep it to myself!
I said I wasn't gonna tell nobody, but I
Couldn't keep it to myself,
What the Lord has done for me!

Verse
You oughta been there
You oughta been there
When He saved my soul
Saved my soul
You oughta been there
You oughta been there
When He put my name on the roll
You know that I
Started walkin'
And I
Started talkin'
Then I
Started singin'
Then I
Started shoutin',
What the Lord has
done for me!

        —Traditional gospel hymn

Contents

Foreword, *by Cornel West*   ix

Introduction   xv

1 Couldn't Keep It to Myself
   Removing My Mask   1

2 What the Lord Has Done for Me
   Black Theology and Black Power   31

3 You Oughta Been There
   A Black Theology of Liberation   51

4 When He Put My Name on the Roll
   Learning from My Critics   85

5 When He Saved My Soul
   Learning from My Students   108

6 I Started Walkin' and Talkin'
   The Cross and the Lynching Tree   126

7 I Started Singin' and Shoutin'
   Learning from Baldwin   144

   Conclusion   170

   Acknowledgments   175

   Index   177

Foreword

My dear brother, James Cone. Words fail. Any language falls short. Yes, he was a world-historical figure in contemporary theology, no doubt about that. A towering prophetic figure engaging in his mighty critiques and indictment of contemporary Christendom from the vantage point of the least of these, no doubt about that. But I think he would want us to view him through the lens of the cross and the blood at the foot of that cross. So, I want to begin with an acknowledgment that James Cone was an exemplary figure in a tradition of a people who have been traumatized for four hundred years but taught the world so much about healing; terrorized for four hundred years and taught the world so much about freedom; hated for four hundred years and taught the world so much about love and how to love. James Cone was a love warrior with an intellectual twist, rooted in gutbucket Jim Crow Arkansas, ended up in the top of the theological world but was never seduced by the idols of the world.

That is who we are talking about.

There is no James Cone without his parents, Lucy and Charlie. In his great *The Cross and the Lynching Tree* (2011)—a text that will last as long as there is an American empire shot

Editor's note: James H. Cone died on April 28, 2018, soon after completing his memoir. This reflection is adapted from the tribute delivered by Cornel West at Dr. Cone's funeral at New York's Riverside Church on May 7, 2018.

through with white supremacy and predatory capitalism and homophobia and transphobia and patriarchy—he concludes the acknowledgments by thanking Lucy and Charlie, because their "amazing love and wonderful humor . . . created a happy home that kept us from hating anybody."

That is an echo of Emmett Till's mother: "I don't have a minute to hate. I'm going to pursue justice for the rest of my life." It's an echo of John Coltrane's *A Love Supreme*; it's an echo of Toni Morrison's *Beloved*; it's an echo of the love-soaked essays of James Baldwin. James Cone stands in a tradition of a people, a great people, with a grand tradition. The Macedonia African Methodist Episcopal Church, the church on the Jim Crow side—the chocolate side—of Bearden, Arkansas, taught that little Negro genius something. He was already fortified before he got to Union Theological Seminary. He had been shaped, he had been molded, he had been challenged, he had been questioned, and he stood tall.

He stood tall and said: *I got something to say to the world and I don't say it on my own. What do I say?* Like the Isley Brothers' "Caravan of Love," a falling in love with truth and the condition of truth, was always to allow suffering to speak, a falling in love with goodness keeping track of the evil, he begins with white supremacy, he wrestles with white supremacy, but he always connected it to others, even if it took him a little while to get there. How come? Because we got too many black folks loving everybody but black people.

He said: *I'm going to start with black people, then I'm going get to the other people.* Nothing wrong with that. That is who he was, but he had been shaped already by his father. In his autobiography, *My Soul Looks Back* (1982), Charlie tells him: *Let me tell you something, James, I'll never allow your mother to work in the white house because I know about sexual violation, I know about harassment, and I don't have that much money, I'm only making a thousand dollars a year, but I'm going out to collect and sell wood every day and I'm not accepting a penny. Don't ever sell your integrity. Don't you ever allow anybody to buy your integrity. You stand tall even if you broke because you got some joy that the world didn't give you and the world can't take away.*

So, when he talked about the Charlie Cone inside of him, that's the Sankofa that our black-nationalist brothers and sisters understand: you better not stand up and move forward until you are connected to the best of what has gone into you, because the highest standards have been set by those who are dead. The question is, Will our lives be connected in any way to the afterlife of our brother Cone as he moves on the other side of the Jordan?

James Cone was not just an academic theologian. He lived life-or-death. His theology was grounded in the cry of black blood, the wailing of black suffering, the moans and groans of black hurt and black pain, and somehow trying to convince us not just to have courage, but fortitude. A Nazi soldier can be courageous and still be a thug; fortitude is courage connected to magnanimity and greatness of character. That is what we are looking at when we see James Cone.

He was a great man, based on biblical criteria. He served, he sacrificed for the least of these, he tried to hold up the bloodstained banner with a level of spiritual nobility and moral royalty already enacted by Lucy, already enacted by Charlie, already enacted by the best of his church; and by the time he began to interact with vanilla brothers and sisters he was misunderstood, he was misconstrued. But just because he was mad and enraged, because he was focusing on the sin, that didn't make him a hater. He had charitable Christian hatred: he hated the sin, but still tried to love the sinner. And the problem is so easy. Others look at black folk and ask, *How come they're so mad? How come they're so angry?* Well, if your children were treated that way, if your children were going to jail, your children were receiving a decrepit education, you'd be upset. But you don't expect us to be upset?

James Cone said, *Let me tell you something right now, I'm not one of those Negroes who is afraid and scared and intimidated. I am going to tell you the truth, and I am going to talk about the suffering of black people.*

He always acknowledged the prophetic white brothers and sisters, such as Donald Shriver, Tom Driver, Christopher Morse, William Hordern, Lester Scherer, Beverly Harrison, Robert Ellsberg; any white brother or sister who approached him as a human being had a chance to experience his tenderness, his sweetness. But he was still on fire!

And that's what we need these days. We need the spirit of the tradition that produced a James Cone in the younger generation: not just on fire, but putting love and justice at the center of it, and, most importantly, willing to take a risk.

In his writing, his discipline was unbelievable: *Black Theology and Black Power* (1969); then here comes *A Black Theology of Liberation* (1970); then *The Spirituals and the Blues* (1972); here comes *God of the Oppressed* (1975); and with Gayraud Wilmore, *Black Theology: A Documentary History* (1979). Then *My Soul Looks Back* (1982); here comes *For My People* (1984); here comes *Speaking the Truth* (1986); here comes *Martin & Malcolm & America* (1991). He said: *Christians, if you don't understand the genius of Malcolm X, go back to the cross.*

Go back to the cross. That's what he was telling us. That's what it is to be on fire. He's still on fire. His spirit will be strong, it will be transfigured, it will be transformed. We will never forget our brother. Let's live our lives in such a way that we remain in the same tradition as our brother James Cone.

Cornel West

Cornel West is Professor of the Practice of Public Philosophy at Harvard University. His many books include Race Matters *and* Black Prophetic Rage. *(This reflection is reprinted with his permission.)*

Introduction

I resisted writing this book. It is hard to tell the truth about yourself. But the more I tried not to write, the more I felt compelled to write. I thought about Fredrick Douglass, Harriet Jacobs, W. E. B. Du Bois, Ida B. Wells-Barnett, and Malcolm X. Autobiography is a medium African Americans have chosen to speak to America, from the slave narratives to the present. I felt the need to speak not so much about myself as about black theology and how it found me and gave me voice. I have tried to tell my story of black theology as truthfully and forcefully as I know how. The journey has been long, sometimes difficult, but always exciting and empowering.

I knew I would be risking a lot to put blackness and faith in conversation. But I had no other choice. I knew faith, but I was just getting acquainted with blackness. And it was disturbing my soul, making me uncomfortable with the faith of the Macedonia AME Church in Bearden, Arkansas. The church where I grew up could not speak to Black Power. It was too outrageous, but that is what attracted me to it.

CHAPTER 1

Couldn't Keep It to Myself

Removing My Mask

When the Detroit rebellion, also known as the "12ᵗʰ Street Riot," broke out in July of 1967, the turmoil woke me out of my academic world. I could no longer continue quietly teaching white students at Adrian College (Michigan) about Karl Barth, Paul Tillich, and other European theologians when black people were dying in the streets of Detroit, Newark, and the back roads of Mississippi and Alabama. I had to do something. But I wasn't a civil rights leader, like Martin Luther King Jr., or an artist, like James Baldwin, who was spurred in his writing when he saw the searing image of a black girl, Dorothy Counts, surrounded by hateful whites as she attempted to integrate a white high school in Charlotte, North Carolina (September 1957). I was a theologian, asking: What, if anything, is theology worth in the black struggle in America?

Theology was my trade—all I had to show for nearly thirty years of living. I had a Ph.D. in systematic theology, but I didn't know how to use it in the fight for justice since nothing I'd read spoke about what black people were going through. I had no models to follow. The few Negroes who had studied theology imitated white theologians, as I'd done, while writing a doctoral dissertation on the Swiss theologian Karl Barth.

The Detroit rebellion deeply troubled me and revolutionized my way of thinking. I could no longer write the same way, following the lead of Europeans and white Americans. I had to find a *new* way of talking about God that was accountable to black people and their fight for justice. I was the only Negro professor at a white college in a Midwestern city of about 25,000 people, which included, as far as I could tell, no more than fifty Negroes, including me.

I had gone to Adrian a "Negro" during the summer of 1966, and I had tried my best to "fit in." Lester B. Scherer, a friend and classmate at Garrett Theological Seminary (now Garrett-Evangelical) and Northwestern University, had recommended me, and I didn't want to disappoint him. He had taken a risk, assuring colleagues who'd never had a Negro on their faculty that I was no troublemaker or angry black militant, and thus would make an excellent hire. Although Stokely Carmichael's proclamation of Black Power was the most talked about subject in the news, I did not talk about race with my neighbors. I kept my cool, trying to be a good Negro; I had a wife and a four-year-old son, and I didn't want to make our social life impossible. I didn't even talk about race with my progressive colleagues at the college. We talked about our classes in religion, literature, and history, limiting our talk of justice to the escalating war in Vietnam. We marched against the war, incurring strong opposition from the president of the college, a Goldwater Republican, whose son was killed in Vietnam. I couldn't separate the killing of colored people in Vietnam from Negroes in America's cities, a connection Martin Luther King Jr. had made in his great "Beyond Vietnam" address at Riverside Church in New York on April 4, 1967. But I saw no way of articulating that connection, without, like King, expressing deep anger about global racism, thereby threatening relations with my white colleagues.

I was also silent about racial issues at the First United Methodist Church I attended. I knew that any talk about racism would be too controversial for white Republican Christians who'd voted for Barry Goldwater, and who were eager to show me, with their smiles and general friendliness, that they were nice people with no prejudice against Negroes. In turn, I wanted to show them that I was a Christian Negro with good manners and no resentment against white people. I quietly blended in, participating as a leader in worship and taking young people on weekend retreats for Bible study and play.

Of course, I had learned as a child to wear a mask, a disguise I had perfected by the time I moved to Adrian. "We wear the mask that grins and lies," wrote the great Negro poet Paul Laurence Dunbar in a poem I began reciting in grade school.[1] Those words spoke to the experience of Negroes in Arkansas and the South generally, who took great risks in disagreeing with whites. When a Negro expressed an opinion that differed from a white person, the typical response

---

1. Paul Laurence Dunbar, "We Wear the Mask" (1895), in Henry Louis Gates and Nellie Y. McKay, eds., *The Norton Anthology of African American Literature* (New York: W. W. Norton, 1997), 896.

was, "Are you calling me a liar, boy?" No black person would dare contradict a white man or woman, or even a child; in their world, white was always right. Knowing that, we had to disguise our true selves in order to keep a job, stay out of jail, or even stay alive. "Got one mind for white folks to see, another for what I know is me"—so went a well-known Negro folk song that I often heard as I was growing up.

As a child, I learned to wear a mask whenever I went to town in Bearden—careful always not to show my real self, for fear of offending white people. When I was around whites, I was mostly silent, spoke only when spoken to, and showed the deference expected of me: head down, never looking any white person in the eyes, for only "uppity niggers" would be so bold. I went to the back door of their homes, drank water from "colored" fountains, addressed whites as Mr. and Mrs., and moved out of their way on the street. I hated what the writer Richard Wright called "The Ethics of Living Jim Crow."[2] But whites were powerful and dangerous, and they could strike without warning; you had to be very careful and watch their every move, lest you unintentionally caused them offense. So I kept my mask on until I got back to "Cotton Belt," the name for the black community where I grew up. There I could relax and exhale a bit, safe from the unpredictable reactions of white folk.

I took my mask with me to graduate school at Garrett and Northwestern. There, too, I was a "good" Negro and for the most part suppressed my rage, with one notable excep-

---

2. Richard Wright, "The Ethics of Living Jim Crow, an Autobiographical Sketch" (1937), in *The Norton Anthology of African American Literature*, 1388–96.

tion. That occurred one day in a class taught by one of my doctoral advisors, Philip S. Watson, a Cambridge-educated Luther scholar and author of *Let God Be God* (1947). A staid, short, gray-haired Englishman, he was an excellent advisor, whose office door was always open to me. I was his favorite student, and other students knew it. But one day in 1961 I completely lost control in class. My anger erupted, stunning Watson and everyone else, including my brother, Cecil, who was sitting beside me.

At that time, sit-ins and Freedom Rides were irrupting all over the South. Black and white activists were being beaten bloody, sometimes killed, for advocating the right to eat at lunch counters, ride on integrated interstate buses, or use public bathrooms. White ministers condemned their actions from their pulpits and in the media, calling such activists "outsider agitators," "communists," "criminals," and "thugs." White theologians, including my advisor and his colleagues, said nothing. They taught as if nothing was happening in the streets of America. My anger had been building for days, months, and even years. I felt that I should be with my brothers and sisters who were actively fighting for black freedom.

"Dr. Watson!" I interrupted him, during a lecture. He stopped and looked at me, obviously irritated.

"What is it?" he asked.

"You are a racist!" I shouted, my voice growing louder. "You have been lecturing for days about the violence of Catholics against Protestants during the sixteenth and seventeenth centuries in Europe, and you've said nothing about the violence of white Protestants against blacks in the South *today!*"

Looking back, I know I should have found a more respectful way to raise my concern. But black pain runs deep, wide, and long, and there were times when I could not contain my rage. Yet Watson, a recent immigrant from England, living in a white area of Evanston, with no contact with Negroes, except five or six students at Garrett, had no understanding of that. All he knew was what he read and heard in the media, which was grossly inadequate and inaccurate. He paced the floor for a few seconds, which seemed liked minutes. The class was silent and I could feel every eye upon me. I realized immediately what I had done. I'd taken off my mask too soon. I was still in graduate school and needed Watson's approval to get my doctorate. Now I had offended him in the worst way.

He turned and looked at me with anger in his piercing eyes, then shouted, "That's simply not true! Class dismissed!" With that he stormed out of the room and headed toward his office. I followed anxiously behind, wondering whether I had lost him forever, and with him my degree.

"Jim, you know I'm not a racist!" he said, after we entered his office. "Yes, I know," I replied. "But Dr. Watson, I wasn't really talking about you, even though my words came out that way. I apologize. I was talking about the deeper problem of race in America, which weighs heavy on my soul, making it difficult for me to study and do my best work."

Surprisingly, he seemed to recognize what I was wrestling with. He relaxed and his anger subsided. For the first and only time we had a long conversation about race. I put my mask back on, and saved my degree.

For about a year after joining the faculty at Adrian College I had done what was expected of a Negro. But then Detroit exploded and so did I. My explosion shook me at the core of my racial identity, killing the "Negro" in me and resurrecting my black self. I felt a *black fire* burning inside me, so hot I couldn't control it any longer. Yet, I had to be careful to keep my rage from exploding among my white colleagues and friends. I withdrew and kept to myself, lamenting over the forty-three dead after five days of black rebellion. But I had to find a way to let it out, to express what I was feeling about blackness and whiteness, race and theology. That was when I knew I had to write to let the world know what was stirring in me or lose my sanity.

In churches and the news media, white ministers and politicians condemned Black Power as hate speech; they denounced urban uprisings as the work of Negro thugs engaged in criminal activity. Many Negro ministers and civil rights activists agreed. I reacted the same way as James Baldwin, whom I'd been reading since graduate school: "Who is looting whom? Grabbing off the TV set? He doesn't really want the TV set. He's saying screw you. . . . He wants to let you know he's there. . . . You are accusing a captive population who has been robbed of everything. . . . I think it's obscene."[3]

Martin Luther King Jr. was greatly disturbed about unrest in the cities and the rhetoric of Black Power, which reminded him of the violent language of Malcolm X. I did not share King's view. Black Power expressed what I had been feeling from the time Stokely Carmichael first shouted the phrase in Mississippi in June 1966. Though it challenged King's nonviolent philosophy, I never thought of Black Power in terms of violence and hate; rather, it expressed the necessity of black people asserting their dignity in the face of 350 years of white

---

3. "An Interview with James Baldwin," *Esquire,* July 1968, 51.

supremacy. Black Power simply meant that Negroes were tired of being exploited and humiliated. As a theologian, I felt compelled to write a manifesto to white churches announcing that Negroes could no longer tolerate the violation of their dignity. I had to give voice to the feelings of rage in the Negro community, and especially the rage inside of me.

I began rereading Malcolm X for a deeper understanding of Black Power, as the response to black self-hate. Malcolm X revolutionized my consciousness, transforming me from a Negro theologian to a *black* theologian, angry and ready to do battle with white theologians. My newfound blackness impelled me to write, to let the world know that a *new* voice had arrived on the theological scene.

I didn't know I could write. I had never written anything, except academic papers about European theologians in graduate school. Black Power, however, was not an academic issue. It was an *existential* issue about black dignity—the political liberation of black people from white oppression "by any means necessary,"[4] as Malcolm X had said.

Writing about Black Power was different from writing about European theologians. For me nothing was at stake in European theology. It didn't matter whether Barth or Harnack was right in their debate about the meaning of revelation. I wasn't ready to risk my life for that. Now with Black Power, everything was at stake—the affirmation of black humanity in a white supremacist world. I was ready to die for black dignity.

---

4. See Malcolm X's address at the "Founding Rally of the Organization of Afro-American Unity" (June 28, 1964), in Malcolm X, *By Any Means Necessary* (New York: Pathfinder, 1970), 84.

I was fed up with white theologians writing about the gospel as if it had nothing to do with Black Power and black people's struggle for cultural identity and political justice. I was fed up with liberal white ministers condemning riots instead of the social conditions that created them. I was fed up with conservative black churches preaching an other-worldly gospel as if Jesus had nothing to say about how white supremacy had created a world that was killing black people. I knew that Black Power advocates, like Stokely Carmichael, and militant black ministers, like Albert Cleage, had no interest in debating white religious scholars or well-schooled white ministers. But I did! It was time for me to join my black brothers and sisters in the fight for justice using what I'd learned in graduate school. It was time to turn the white man's theology against him and make it speak for the liberation of black people. Militant Negro ministers needed a theology that could liberate their minds from any dependence on white theology.

"Black Power is the gospel of Jesus in America today!" That was my central theological claim as I reflected on the Detroit rebellion. I couldn't stop thinking about it. I went to bed thinking about it, got up in the morning thinking about it, and thought about it all day. I was obsessed. It was like a revelation, a sudden bolt from the blue, a fire burning inside me. I didn't say a word to anybody about what I was feeling and thinking. There was nobody I could talk to about it in Adrian, not even my friend Lester Scherer. I simply meditated on the claim for months, examining it over and over again in my mind, thinking about its truth and wondering why I hadn't thought of it before. Then, to my surprise, I boldly asserted it in a theological discussion with white friends from graduate school at the annual meeting of the American Academy of Religion in November 1967.

"Black Power is not the gospel!," they replied with great emphasis, nearly in unison. "How in the world could you assert such an outrageous, nonsensical idea?," asked Ronald Goetz, a well-known scholar of Karl Barth at Garrett and my closest friend in theology. He viewed my claim as an ideological distortion of the gospel; as he saw it, following Barth, who himself was following the great Danish theologian, Søren Kierkegaard, God's revelation is "wholly other," never, ever identified with the ideas and actions of human beings.

I understood Goetz's concern because I too had studied Barth and Kierkegaard. At Garrett, we'd allied ourselves against the liberal theologies of Schleiermacher, Ritschl, and Harnack. One needed only look at what happened to the German churches during the Nazi era to see the dangers of identifying God with human actions. Barth's "No! answer to Emil Brunner" on natural theology and his bold "Barmen Declaration" (1934)[5] made clear the dangers of a theology of culture. I was well aware of Goetz's concern, that God's power and human power are not the same. But I was thinking about God from the bottom and not the top, from the experience of the powerless black oppressed and not from that of the powerful white oppressor. God's power is found in human weakness, the struggle of the oppressed against their oppressors. It was clear to me that those who condemned Black Power were blind to the ideological dan-

---

5. See Gary Dorrien, *The Barthian Revolt in Modern Theology: Theology Without Weapons* (Louisville, KY: Westminster John Knox, 2000), 122–28; Eberhard Busch, *The Barmen Theses: Then and Now* (Grand Rapids, MI: Eerdmans, 2010).

gers present in white evangelical, liberal and neo-orthodox theologies in America that either embraced or ignored the role of white supremacist ideals in their churches.

This point was clear to me in my *gut* before I could articulate it with my mind. For most evangelicals, revelation was found in the inerrant scriptures, and one need not look elsewhere. I knew in my gut that God's revelation was found among poor black people.

Though he disagreed with me, Ronald Goetz could tell that I was dead serious, not engaging in theological hyperbole. He said, "If you believe that, Jim, why don't you say it publicly in writing and in a carefully worked out argument?" He challenged me to give a public lecture on the theme of "Christianity and Black Power" at Elmhurst College (near Chicago), where he was teaching.

I gladly accepted Goetz's challenge because it was what I needed to organize my thoughts. He also gave me an audience where my thinking could be tested. Now I had to make an intelligent theological argument and not simply assert something because it was emotionally satisfying. I had to back up my claim with a thoughtful reflection. It was one thing to say simply that Black Power is the gospel, and quite another to make a credible theological argument for linking the two. No one, not even militant Negro ministers, had even thought about joining Black Power with Jesus. Their thinking was somewhat like that of Barth, who declared an "infinite qualitative distinction between God and the human being." God is in heaven and we are on earth, Barth claimed, and any suggestion of a likeness between God and human beings is anathema. No Negro preacher would dispute that assertion, and their congregations would follow suit.

Yet Black Power advocates, following Malcolm X, rejected the Christian faith. Like Malcolm, they said, "Christianity is the white man's religion." They saw Jesus as a blond, blue-eyed white man. Militant Negro ministers who wanted to embrace blackness struggled with how to reconcile Black Power and the gospel, Malcolm and Martin, self-defense and nonviolence, liberation and reconciliation. Faced with the choice of embracing blackness or Christian faith, a few preachers chose blackness, left the church, and joined the Nation of Islam or some other non-Christian black religion.

Blackness spoke to the soul of black being-in-the-world, and no one had articulated blackness better than Malcolm. "We are black first and everything else second," he had declared. Martin King, meanwhile, was uncomfortable with talk of blackness; he remained a Negro all his life and only reluctantly used the word "black" when pressured by black militants. He would not talk publicly or even privately with Malcolm, and he pleaded with Carmichael to stop talking about Black Power. King saw Black Power as alienating Negroes from whites, thereby making it impossible for the two communities to work together to create an integrated society.

If I were going to demonstrate *theologically* that "the message of Black Power is the message of Christ," I first had to define what I meant by Black Power, and then by the message of Christ. To define Black Power, I turned first to Stokely Carmichael, its chief, best-known, and most controversial advocate. He was the public symbol of Black Power and he had given many speeches on its meaning. He had also expanded on the theme in a book written with Charles V. Hamilton, a black professor of political science at Columbia

University, *Black Power: The Politics of Liberation*. With the persuasive power of his rhetoric, Carmichael redefined the black struggle for justice, placing black self-determination at its center. "The goal of black self-determination and black self-identity—Black Power—is full participation in the decision-making processes affecting the lives of black people, and recognition of the virtues in themselves as black people."[6] Who could disagree with that?

Even more important than Carmichael for my thinking, however, was the work of other writers: Malcolm's *Autobiography* (1965), James Baldwin's *Nobody Knows My Name* (1961) and "The Fire Next Time" (1963), Richard Wright's *Native Son* (1940) and *Black Boy* (1945), Albert Camus's *The Plague* (1948) and *The Rebel* (1956), and Franz Fanon's, *The Wretched of the Earth* (1966) and *Black Skin White Masks* (1967). These writers inspired me to do in theology what they did in literature.

Far more important than any writer, though, was the *black fire* burning inside me and demanding expression. The spirit of blackness was driving me crazy in a good way, making me laugh and cry, walk and run, and even sing and dance as I listened to the sound and moved to the rhythm of Aretha's "Respect" and James Brown's "Say It Loud—I'm Black and I'm Proud." I began wearing dashikis, raised my Black Power fist, and adopted an Afro hairstyle so people could see that I was *Black*. I began reading the young black poets, like LeRoi Jones's (Amiri Baraka), *Preface to a Twenty Volume Suicide Note . . .* (1957), *The Dead Lecturer* (1964), and *Home: Social Essays* (1966); Don Lee's (Haki Madhubuti) *Black Pride* (1968),

---

6. Stokely Carmichael and Charles V. Hamilton, *Black Power: The Politics of Liberation in America* (New York: Vintage Book, 1967), 47.

and Nikki Giovanni's *Black Feeling Black Talk Black Judgment* (1968). I heard them read their poetry before they published. They were like traveling evangelists, going from city to city all over the United States, giving poetic sermons, urging black people to *"think black!"* (Don L. Lee, 1967) because *We a' BaddDDD People* (Sonia Sanchez, 1970). The black poet Dudley Randall, of Broadside Press (Detroit), published their poems in pamphlets and books, and churches and community centers provided a place for them to read their poetry. Their powerful verses turned me on, reminding me of the best in black preaching. They could make blackness sing and dance. People shouted "Right on, Sister!" "Say it, Brother!" "Yeah, you talking!" I felt like I was in church—which I was, the church of blackness.

I also went to hear the Rev. Albert Cleage preach a Black Power gospel at the Shrine of the Black Madonna in Detroit. He was the author of *The Black Messiah* (1968), a book of sermons addressed to Black Power advocates, trying to persuade them to stay in the church, with titles like "An Epistle to Stokely" and "Brother Malcolm." He was the only preacher I heard who had the courage to be unashamedly and unapologetically black. I immersed myself in talk about black love, black unity, and black pride, black liberation, and the black revolution. The meaning of Black Power was clear: the self-determination of black people in every area of their lives by any means they deemed necessary. No one outside of the black struggle for justice could tell us what we could and couldn't say or do to gain our freedom. Not even Negroes!

I began to read the Bible through the lens of Black Power, black arts, and the black consciousness movement. A revolutionary Jesus leaped off the pages of scripture into my mind, enabling me to see things I had not seen before. Luke's Jesus, citing the great prophet Isaiah, proclaimed:

> The Spirit of the Lord is upon me,
> because he has anointed me to preach good news
>   to the poor.
> He has sent me to proclaim release to the captives
>   and
> recovering of sight to the blind,
> to set at liberty those who are oppressed,
> to proclaim the acceptable year of the Lord.
>   (4:18-19 RSV; Isaiah 61:1)

Luke's Gospel was clear: Jesus's ministry was essentially liberation on behalf of the poor and the oppressed. I didn't need a doctorate in theology to know that liberation defined the heart of Jesus's ministry. Black people had been preaching and singing about it for centuries. When I turned away from white theology and back to scripture and the black religious experience, the connection between Black Power and the gospel of Jesus became crystal clear. Both were concerned about the liberation of the oppressed. In fact, the actions, songs, and preaching of the civil rights movement, with Martin Luther King Jr. as its central spokesperson, expressed liberation in bus boycotts, sit-ins, marches, and Freedom Rides. King's civil rights movement was a liberation movement that challenged the American empire. The only thing missing in the Negro freedom struggle was the accent on blackness and the right of black people to assert their dignity without compromise. Negro churches, ministers, and activists rejected blackness because they did not want to alienate whites, who interpreted Christianity as universal (which for them, of course, meant white), and thus were opposed to the particularity of blackness, which they often identified with sin and evil, even the devil. But I contended that the gospel of Jesus is not opposed to blackness. On the contrary, Christ is black! —that is, identified with the black struggle for justice and dignity.

I became intellectually comfortable writing about Jesus's gospel without needing the support of white biblical scholars and systematic theologians to validate my perspective. Reading them took me away from the biblical Jesus to a white Jesus of their creation. I remembered sitting in New Testament classes at Garrett where professors presented Jesus as a white man. How could Jesus be white, since he was born a Jew in Palestine, "under a very hot sun," as James Baldwin reminded the World Council of Churches?[7] It made no sense to anyone who knew anything about the Middle East. The real historical Jesus, whom scholars have been seeking since the eighteenth century, was *not* white. That much I knew. When it became clear to me that Jesus was not biologically white and that white scholars actually lied by *not* telling people who he really was, I stopped trusting anything they said. It was ideologically tainted. I began to trust my own black experience as a better source for knowledge about God and Jesus. The black religious experience was less ideologically tainted because blacks were powerless and could not impose their view of Jesus on anybody. But often blacks mis-

7. James Baldwin, "White Racism or World Community?" (1968), in *Collected Essays*, ed. Toni Morrison (New York: Library of America, 1998), 749.

trusted their own experience, turned instead to whites for their values, using the same white portraits of Jesus in their homes and in the stained-glass windows in their churches.

"One writes out of one thing only—one's own experience,"[8] wrote James Baldwin. When I started to trust my experience, I began with verve and self-confidence to write my first essay, "Christianity and Black Power" (1968).[9] "If the gospel is the liberation for the oppressed," I wrote, "then Jesus is where the oppressed are—proclaiming release to the captives." I also emphasized the prophets' call for justice, which prefigured Jesus's solidarity with the poor. I quoted sixteenth-century reformer Martin Luther, Swiss theologian Karl Barth, and French existentialist philosopher Albert Camus to show that I was academically informed in theology and philosophy. I made them say what I wanted to say, even though I knew that they probably would reject the blackness I saw in the gospel of Jesus. But I still had a lot of intellectual work to do if I expected to be taken seriously. My idea of liberation was in its early stages of development.

In February 1968 I gave my first public lecture at Elmhurst College. From Ron Goetz and other faculty and students in the college community, all of whom were white, I received creative and critical responses. I have always liked critical debates, and have enjoyed representing the minority, unpopular view, especially in defense of black dignity. In this case, the debate was intense but respectful. The audience, as expected, challenged my identification of Black

---

8. "Autobiographical Notes," in *Collected Essays*, 8.

9. See James H. Cone, "Christianity and Black Power," in *The Risks of Faith: The Emergence of A Black Theology of Liberation, 1968–1998* (Boston: Beacon Press, 1999), 3–12.

Power with the gospel today. "Blacks are not the only people suffering and liberation is not the only message of the gospel." These two points were typical responses from white audiences. Of course, I never said that blacks were the only people suffering or that liberation was the only message in the Bible. But I replied that white supremacy is America's original sin and liberation is the Bible's central message. Any theology in America that fails to engage white supremacy and God's liberation of black people from that evil is not Christian theology but a theology of the Antichrist.

My language was offensive, and I knew it. The truth of the gospel is always offensive and unpopular because it expresses solidarity with the powerless and those on the margins. Jesus was offensive to the Roman government and that was why they crucified him. If we are going to understand and embrace his liberating message today, we must see Jesus through the experience of the oppressed black people who are crying out for justice in a white racist society.

Later in February I went to Cincinnati for the organizing meeting of the Black Methodists for Church Renewal (BMCR), a radical group in the United Methodist Church who wrote "The Black Paper," expressing their solidarity with Black Power and the black revolution. Borrowing a well-known phrase from a white theologian, Paul Lehmann of Union Theological Seminary (New York),[10] they said that Black Power "is a call to respond to God's action in history, which is to make and keep human life human." They did not say that Black Power is the gospel because that would

---

10. See Paul Lehmann, *Ethics in a Christian Context* (Louisville, KY: Westminster John Knox Press, 1963).

have raised a red flag in a white church. Nothing about God could be called black without controversy. But they affirmed as much of the spirit of Black Power as they could. It was similar to an earlier statement on Black Power by an ad hoc National Committee of Negro Churchmen (later called National Conference of Black Churchmen), published in the *New York Times* on July 31, 1966, about a month following Stokely Carmichael's proclamation of Black Power during the Meredith March in Mississippi on June 17. It acknowledged the need for Black Power because "powerlessness breeds a race of beggars."[11] I thought both statements fell short of what needed to be said. Black people needed a *theological* revolution that could stand alongside Black Power and the black arts movement. We needed a revolution in thinking about the Christian gospel and not just an emotional embrace of blackness.

C. Eric Lincoln, author of the classic *The Black Muslims in America* (1961), then professor of sociology and religion at Union Theological Seminary in New York, was the keynote speaker in Cincinnati. He was the most respected and well-known scholar of black religion. I was in awe of him, not because of his religious and political perspective but because of his scholarly achievements. He was also physically a large man, and I felt small in his presence. Though I was shy about introducing myself, Negail Riley, a friend and pastor of the Wesley United Methodist Church (Little Rock, Arkansas) urged me to share my essay with him.

---

11. See James H. Cone and Gayraud S. Wilmore, eds., *Black Theology: A Documentary History, Volume I: 1966–1979* (Maryknoll, NY: Orbis Books, 1993), 19.

"Do you think he would be interested in reading it?" I asked.

"Of course!" he said.

I was concerned because I knew my black perspective was much more radical than Lincoln's. He, like King, was an integrationist, and while I didn't reject integration, my thinking and spirit were much closer to Malcolm and black nationalism. While I didn't tell Riley about my political concerns, I continued asking questions that also showed my intellectual insecurity.

"Do you think it's good enough?"

"Don't worry, it's a good piece of writing," he replied.

Reluctantly, I gave my essay to Riley for Lincoln to read, hoping he was at least black enough to give me a fair reading.

After about an hour, Lincoln sent for me to come to his hotel room. I felt uneasy—as if summoned by my father, not knowing whether I was to receive praise or scorn. I made my way to Lincoln's room and he beckoned me to sit down. I could barely keep from shaking.

"You have written a very good essay," he said. "It is what the black and white church communities need at this moment in American history."

I could hardly believe what I heard. "You really think so?" I asked.

"Absolutely!" he told me. "I wouldn't say it if I didn't think so. In fact, you have a promising future as a theologian, and I look forward to reading more of what you write." He suggested that I send it to *Motive* magazine, a United Methodist publication, as well as *The Christian Century*. These were the most widely read journals by theologians, pastors, laypersons, seminary and college students.[12] And then for several hours, like a father to a son, he spoke to me about my essay and about what it means to be a scholar.

James Baldwin said, "If you are going to be a writer there is nothing I can say to stop you; if you're not going to be a writer nothing I can say will help you. What you really need at the beginning is somebody to let you know that the effort is real."[13] Lincoln couldn't have stopped me. Nobody had that power. I was too obsessed with my calling to be a theological witness to the black freedom struggle. Nor did I need him to help me figure out what I wanted to say. Lincoln was, and remained, an integrationist, while I was forging a new path inspired by Black Power. What Lincoln did was let me know that my effort was worth doing—an assurance I definitely needed.

I told Lincoln that I was going to expand my essay into a book during the summer. He looked at me with an encouraging smile but also with a facial expression that said I might be biting off more than I could chew. He nodded, as if to say "show me what you can do." I thanked him for taking the time to read my essay and for his words of encouragement, and then we said goodbye.

I drove my new 1968 light blue Saab back toward Adrian, thinking about Lincoln's inspiring words and the book I was going to write. I was excited about the intellectual

---

12. I sent my essays to *Motive* and *The Christian Century*, but they sent nice letters of rejection. I was not deterred.

13. "The Art of Fiction LXXVIII: James Baldwin," an interview by Jordan Elgrably and George Plimpton, in *Conversations with James Baldwin*, ed. Fred L. Standley and Louis H. Pratt (Jackson: University Press of Mississippi, 1989), 251.

challenge before me. When you write, you need to know *who* you are writing for and *what* message you want to deliver to them and *why* you feel the need to say what you've got to say. I was writing to and for *poor* black Christians who had been humiliated in white society and rendered invisible in white theology. My message to blacks was: "It is time to stop hating who you are. God created you black—love yourself, love your hands and face, big nose and lips, for that is the only way you can love God. Blackness is God's gift to humanity."

I was also writing to white people, especially white churches and their theologians. I had to tell them that their white Christianity was *not* the gospel of Jesus. White supremacy, in fact, is the Antichrist! I couldn't wait to make my case, for the sake of the gospel and the humanity of black people.

However, as a theologian, I had a consciousness that I was also writing to oppressed peoples all over the world. I wanted to be an example of what they could do in their own situations. They no longer had to be silent about who they were. Just as I spoke and wrote about blackness, they could speak and write about their identity, too. The particularity of blackness reached beyond itself and joined the struggles of poor people all over the world.

Along with Lincoln, there were many other people who let me know that my intellectual effort was worthwhile, even from my childhood in Bearden. Everything started with the profound love of my parents, Lucy and Charlie, who assured their sons, Charles, Cecil, and me, that with education, hard work, and discipline, we could achieve great things in life, despite the barriers of white supremacy. Dostoevsky's

Alyosha, in *The Brothers Karamazov,* was right when he told the young boys gathered around him:

> You must know that there is nothing higher, or stronger, or sounder, or more useful afterwards in life, than some good memory, especially a memory from childhood, from the parental home. You hear a lot said about your education, yet some such beautiful, sacred memory, preserved from childhood, is perhaps the best education. If a man stores up many such memories to take into life, then he is saved for his whole life.[14]

I have many sacred memories of my parents who loved me and protected me from the worst of white supremacy and empowered me to believe in myself. They gave their sons the "best education," which has sustained me throughout my professional career. They told their sons it was up to us to prove that what whites said about us was a lie, as many Negroes before had done in every area of life. It was our responsibility to develop our fullest intellectual potential. We owed it not only to ourselves but also to our community, and to humanity, to become the best we could be.

Their lessons took root. My late brother Cecil received his Ph.D. from Emory University in systematic theology, wrote a book on the *Identity Crisis in Black Theology* (1975), which incidentally contained a sharp critique of my perspective on black theology, and ultimately became the president of Edward Waters College in Jacksonville, Florida. My oldest

---

14. Fyodor Dostoevsky, *The Brothers Karamazov,* trans. Richard Pevear and Larissa Volokhonsky (New York: Farrar, Straus & Giroux, 1990), 774.

brother, Charles, earned a master's degree in education, became a teacher and then a principal in Pine Bluff, Arkansas, and gave to his staff, his teachers, and his sixth-grade students the best of what was given to him.

Whatever success I achieved as a writer and professor began with my parents, but it also depended on other people—too many to name. I view the people who nurtured me as gifts from God. I think of my teachers in elementary and high school who gave me much love and all the knowledge in books and life they had, always reinforcing what my parents said and encouraging me to set no limits on what I could achieve. Mrs. Mildred W. McKinney, nearing a century in age, who taught me in high school, wrote recently to tell me, "I have known from many years ago that you would become a great man, someone who would have the eyes and ears of the world looking and listening to what you had to say! I am blessed to be alive to see and hear and read some of your work."[15] Another high school teacher, Miss Kirby, as I knew her then, drove nearly a hundred miles to hear me speak on black liberation theology in Tacoma, Washington, and stayed on to describe to me and a mostly white audience the intellectual discipline she had seen in me, early on, as her student in Bearden.

I received the same inspiration from Macedonia AME Church and the entire Negro community. "With God nothing is impossible" was the central message. I believed! People are defined by their roots. My roots are in Bearden, but they also go back to slavery and the slave ships, all the way

---

15. November 27, 2016. She was nearly ninety-seven when she wrote me this letter.

back to Africa. I drew on this great resistance heritage when I began to write black theology. Without probing this black heritage, I would have no knowledge of myself.

At Shorter, a small AME Church Junior College, many teachers rewarded me for making an effort to become the best I could be. They were not the best trained academically, but they gave me what I most needed at the time—confidence in my intellectual potential. I read Homer's two epic poems, the *Iliad* and the *Odyssey,* and Plato's *Republic* and *Apology,* and other ancient texts. They whet my appetite to pursue further studies.

In Bearden white people frowned on Negroes who sought an education, especially beyond high school; less was always better. I didn't meet a white person who acknowledged my humanity until I met James and Alice Boyack, married professors of religion and philosophy at Philander Smith College. Both treated me like a human being and taught me a deeper love of the intellectual life. They gave me books to read and invited me to their home for meals and conversation about religion and philosophy. Following a car accident, James Boyack was confined to a wheelchair, and I used to wheel him around the campus, appreciating the opportunity to talk with him about issues in religion and philosophy. We talked about French philosopher René Descartes' "Cogito ergo sum" (I think, therefore I am) and the Scottish philosopher David Hume's refutation of the teleological argument for God's existence from design. We also discussed the German philosophers, Kant's "categorical imperative," and Hegel's idealism. No college professor was more important in inspiring me to believe in my intellectual potential. I wrote my first and only essay in college on the problem of theodicy, exploring the question, "Why do people suffer?" I became obsessed with the question, reading personalists like Edgar S. Brightman and Peter A. Bertocci, both of whom had taught Martin Luther King Jr. at Boston University. Since I came from a people with a long history of suffering, the question of evil and its meaning consumed me. The lynching of fourteen-year-old Emmett Till in 1955 in Mississippi made suffering very real. After all, I was only seventeen and living in a lynching state. I could not stop thinking that the same thing could happen to me. If God loves Negroes, as we claim in church, why are they still being lynched all over the United States? That was my question. At seventeen, I had no answers. But James and Alice Boyack helped me to navigate this intellectual terrain.

It was transforming to meet white people who were kind human beings. My mother always told me they existed, but it had been difficult to believe without experience to validate what she said. James and Alice Boyack were the proof I needed. They also served as my advisors, which is why I went on to Garrett for the bachelor of divinity program.

After my experience with the Boyacks I was not surprised when I met a few professors and students in graduate school who treated me with respect, but I was shocked when most did not. I had to steel myself to deal with them. I had always thought that northern whites were not racist, like their southern counterparts. I believed the myth that "Negroes are free up North." It didn't take me long to see how wrong I was.

Yet at Garrett I was introduced to the exciting world of ideas, for which the Boyacks had prepared me. I encountered many theologians and controversies I had never heard of before. I loved biblical studies, especially the historical critical method, and the quest for the historical Jesus. I read the writings of Rudolph Bultmann, Ernst Käsemann, and Joachim Jeremias. The history of Christianity was an exciting journey, meeting Clement and Origen, Athanasius and Arius, Augustine and the Donatists, Luther, Calvin, and Wesley. I also loved encountering the Western philosophical world that I first met at Philander, from Plato and Aristotle to Nietzsche and Heidegger. But theology was and remains my favorite subject, and that was due to William E. Hordern, the most creative and exciting teacher I've known. He could make complex ideas plain and relevant, and I loved debating theology with him, especially Barth, Tillich, and Niebuhr. I would not have been accepted to the doctoral program at Garrett and Northwestern without the support of Hordern, who also became one of my advisors. I did not have stellar grades when I applied, because it took me a year to manage the academic expectations at Garrett, barely passing my courses, making three Cs my first quarter. But Hordern was not deterred. He emphasized my intellectual potential and passionately advocated for my acceptance.

When I asked for an application to the doctoral program, the professor who was director of graduate studies, a southerner from Virginia, told me I didn't need one because I wouldn't be accepted. "Don't waste your time," he told me. "There are many students from Yale and Harvard with far superior grades than yours." I was deeply hurt but not surprised, since his racism was well known throughout the Garrett community. He seemed to get a great deal of satisfaction dismissing me from his office. I could see the gleam in his eyes. But since I knew Professor Hordern wanted to work with me, I was not defeated. When I told Hordern what had happened, he said angrily, "If you are not accepted in the Ph.D. program in systematic theology, I will resign." The Garrett administration and faculty were not about to let Hordern leave because he was the most widely known and prolific scholar on the faculty. I have often wondered what would have happened to me without Hordern's support. He had more confidence in my academic ability than I did myself. I was determined to show him that he hadn't made a mistake. I don't think anyone worked as hard as I did to prove myself worthy.

I had difficulty writing and was not sure that I could ever become a published scholar like Hordern. My other doctoral advisor, Philip S. Watson, seldom awarded me a grade higher than A-, and always with the comment "only just." He repeatedly told me, "Jim, you need to work on your writing." He was right, of course, and I was helped by his repeated reminder. We talked about it often. I had written only one paper in college and knew almost nothing about writing. In the Negro community we talked and preached, even in college. So, I hardly knew how the English language functioned when words were put on paper. I purchased a ninth-grade English text and studied closely for the first time the various aspects of the language, its rhythm and beauty.

Learning to write well became an obsession as I began to read the essays of James Baldwin, a master of the English language. Baldwin only finished high school, yet he became one of the greatest prose writers in the twentieth century. It took him ten years to write his first novel, *Go Tell It on the Mountain*. He just kept writing and tearing up pages. Richard Wright, who inspired Baldwin, only finished the eighth grade, and his novel *Native Son* shook America at its racist roots. Baldwin and Wright and other creative writers became my inspiration to work hard to realize my intellectual potential as a writer. I knew that there was a lot of undeveloped potential in me, and that it was "up to me," as Baldwin often said, to define myself and reject any white definitions of who I was. I took a class in Greek, starting at the bottom but soon moving to the top of the class, ultimately winning the "Greek Prize" for being the best student at Garrett and becoming a teaching assistant in Greek. Studying Greek, and then German and French, helped me to see how the English language functioned, learning to understand how the placement of words in a sentence affects the meaning.

No one helped me learn to write with facility and precision more than Lester B. Scherer—classmate, friend, and colleague. He read and made editorial suggestions about nearly everything I wrote from the "Christianity and Black Power" essay to *Martin & Malcolm & America* (1991). He talked about the need to eliminate repetition and clean up wordy sentences, reminding me that "less is more." It didn't take me long to realize that a good writer needs a good editor, and that careful revision is essential.

Yet the interracial aspect of our relationship was not easy to navigate. Lester was a well-meaning friend, but his isolation in a white world prevented him from feeling black hurt, a pain so deep that it nearly drives blacks crazy. Lester knew well the history of the slave trade, slavery, segregation, and lynching. He even wrote a good book on *Slavery and the Churches* (1975). It gave me an opportunity to assist him the way he had helped me. But he had no passion for his subject or for writing, and I don't think he ever really understood the depth of black suffering that produced my work.

"What I write," as Claude McKay said, "is urged out of my blood," and in my case out of the blood of blacks in Bearden and elsewhere who saw what I saw, felt what I felt, and loved what I loved. I often thought of what my mother and father and other blacks in Bearden had to go through, and what they might have become in a world without white supremacy. It made me weep, especially when I realized that there were tens of millions of black lives damaged and cut short during four centuries of white supremacy. The more I read about black history the more I felt a pain too deep for words. Could white people ever be made to truly understand the price blacks paid for their privilege?

Like most whites, Lester and his family seemed unaffected by black suffering, and uninterested in the struggles of blacks for justice. He read and edited all my books but nothing of what I said seemed to sink in. I wanted to ask Lester what Juanita, a character in Baldwin's play *Blues for Mr. Charlie*, asked a sympathetic white liberal character: "How can you not know all the things you do not know?"[16] But I didn't ask that. It would have ended our friendship—as would eventually happen, unfortunately, many years later. Instead, most of the time I was patient. I masked my deepest feelings. But I couldn't always do that and sometimes I spoke back harshly. So we avoided race as much as possible.

When I picked up my pen to write "Christianity and Black Power," I vowed that I'd never wear a mask again when black dignity was at stake.

---

16. James Baldwin, *Blues for Mr. Charlie* (New York: Dell, New Laurel edition, 1964), 106.

CHAPTER 2

What the Lord Has Done for Me

Black Theology and Black Power

Soon after I arrived back in Adrian, elated by the encounter with Lincoln, I received a telephone call from the dean of Colgate Rochester Divinity School (Rochester, New York), inviting me to present a lecture and interview for a possible teaching appointment in theology. I was excited about the possibility of teaching theology in graduate school. Black students were demanding the appointment of a black professor who represented their intellectual and spiritual interests in black church studies. C. Eric Lincoln had recommended me, another indication of his belief in my promise. The invitation provided another context to test my theology—this time at a divinity school where Walter Rauschenbusch, creator of the social gospel, had taught, where Howard Thurman, the great Negro prophetic mystic who authored more than twenty books, had received his graduate degree, and where Malcolm X had lectured three days before his assassination in 1965.

I arrived at Colgate in March 1968, ready to debate Black Power and the gospel of Jesus with students and faculty. It was a challenging and exciting time as I developed my theological perspective through intense debate. Theologies develop in response to questions arising out of specific intellectual, political, and religious situations. I was responding to the situation created by the black freedom movement, especially as defined by Martin Luther King Jr. and Malcolm X—the movements for civil rights and Black Power. I felt I was representing not only black people and Lincoln but also myself. I didn't want to disappoint.

Black students were enthralled by my lecture. White faculty and students seemed more amazed by my self-assurance, and they asked the same kinds of questions I had received at Elmhurst College and have continued to receive throughout my career. I was surprised at what white people seemed to hear in my lectures. When I spoke of loving blackness and embracing Black Power, they heard hate toward white people. Malcolm X, Stokely Carmichael, and James Baldwin confronted similar reactions. Any talk about the love and beauty of blackness seemed to arouse fear and hostility in whites.

Blackness in theology was especially troublesome for whites. "What about love and reconciliation?" they repeatedly asked. "Yeah, what about it?" I shot back, speaking in a black vernacular, my natural style. "Loving black people doesn't mean hating white people. Why do black people have to hate themselves to love white people? That's crazy," I said, with much passion, but always with a smile to soften my anger. "The problem is that white people are used to obedient, subservient Negroes, passive Negroes, head down and grinning Negroes. Yet I have to say that day is over and done with. We are in a new day, one in which black people are not turning the other cheek when insulted or consulting white theologians for the last word about the meaning of the Christian gospel. It's time to turn to the religious faith created out of black suffering and dismiss privileged white Christianity and its theology as heresy. What is needed is a black theology, a theology accountable to the black struggle for dignity." This was the first time I started to use the phrase "black theology."

Needless to say, I didn't get the job in theology. Instead they offered me a job in field education, which I refused. Nevertheless, I was deeply pleased with the response of the faculty and students, especially blacks, to my lecture. I told the faculty that I was going to write a book during the summer dealing with black theology. I could tell that they were surprised again by my self-confidence. "Who is this guy?" I could feel them asking. But they invited me back to present four lectures in December as a theological fellow. The invitation gave me extra motivation to write my book.

An additional motivation happened about two weeks later, on April 4, 1968, when Martin Luther King Jr. was shot on the balcony of the Lorraine Motel in Memphis. I heard the news as I was teaching a class in my home on existentialist philosophy. When my wife, Rose, quietly and painfully told me what had happened, I stopped, dazed by the news, collected myself, and calmly, but with a heavy heart, dismissed my students. I didn't want to be around white people. I needed to be alone to assess the meaning of this tragedy.

The King assassination was a turning point in my life. As long as King was alive I had hope that white America could be converted to seeing Negroes as human beings. Without King, where was the hope? Malcolm repeatedly told King and the Negro masses that white America had no conscience and would never treat blacks as human beings unless we forced them. Malcolm's words were ringing true.

I felt that white liberals had killed King, helped by those Negroes who thought he was moving too fast. Even though they didn't pull the trigger, they had refused to listen to King when he proclaimed God's judgment on America for failing to deal with the three great evils of our time: poverty, racism, and war. The white liberal media demonized King, accusing him of meddling in America's foreign affairs by opposing the Vietnam War and blaming him for provoking violence wherever he led a march. White liberals, however, accepted no responsibility for King's murder, and they refused to understand why Negroes were rioting and burning down their communities.

I didn't want to talk to white people about King's assassination or about the uprisings in the cities; it was too much of an emotional burden to explain racism to racists, and I had nothing to say to them. I decided to have my say in writing. I'd give them something to read and talk about. When white friends in Adrian spoke to me, I would sometimes just stare back, without saying a word. If I did speak, what emerged was a caustic word from an "angry black man." They had to know I was not the same, even though I wasn't going to waste time and energy trying to explain myself. People started whispering: "What's wrong with Jim?" I taught my classes, went home to my "Blue Room" in the basement, furiously scribbled notes, and thought deeply about what I was going to write.

As I wrote, I listened to black music—the sonorous sounds of Mahalia Jackson and B. B. King, Aretha Franklin and Bobby "Blue" Bland. They soothed my spiritual and existential pain and took me back to the juke joints and churches in Bearden. That was my world, and I could hear people talking and singing about sorrow and joy in all of life's dimensions. It was what got them through troubled times. I had to write to make sense out of King's assassination, the urban uprisings, the theology I had studied at Garrett, and the life I had lived growing up in Bearden—a world defined both by white supremacy and by the profound black spiritual resistance it provoked. As I reflected on the black experience I soon found the language for writing about Black Power and Christianity. Writing was not only possible but also necessary for my sanity. And as I started to write, I could feel the beat of the spirituals and the blues, a language and sound that spoke to my soul, my yearning to go home, to be with the black people I knew and who knew and loved me, when I hardly knew my name. After living in a wasteland in a Midwestern city, I was starving for cultural and spiritual food. I couldn't wait to get out of Adrian so I could write the book that was burning inside me.

As soon as the semester was over, I left Adrian for home—Bearden and Little Rock. James Baldwin had to leave home and go to Paris to discover who he was to write his first novel, but I had to go back home to Arkansas to write my first book, *Black Theology and Black Power* (1969). My late brother, Cecil, then pastor of Union AME Church (Little Rock), let me use his church office to write. I wrote my heart out, from 7:00 a.m. to 12:00 a.m. every day except Sundays. On Sundays I would stay all day at church services, listening to my brother preach and the congregation sing, pray, and testify, reminding me what I was writing about and for whom I was writing.

Writing my first book was the most liberating experience I've ever had. I felt that I had been waiting all my life for this, to take off my mask and tell white folk—especially my former professors at Garrett and Northwestern—what I really thought. I had listened to them insult and ignore me for so long, treating me and other black students as if we, along with our history and culture, were unimportant. They regarded Africa as having no history and black religious history in the United States as unworthy of mention. This was payback time.

As I started writing, words just flowed out so easily that I could hardly write fast enough. I was in my culture, swimming in words like a fish in water. It was an amazing experience, something I had never felt before. In graduate school, I didn't really know what I was doing, trying to write essays about European theologians who didn't know or care about black people, any more than I cared about them. But now I came alive, with ideas about blackness and liberation, writing about something that mattered.

Demonstrating that Black Power is the gospel in America today was exciting and challenging. It gave me an opportunity to define Black Power as black people asserting the humanity that white supremacy denied. Oppression in any form was a denial of a people's humanity, and the oppressed must use whatever *power* they have to defend their humanity. Defending one's humanity against an oppressive political system was not only a human but a Christian responsibility. Indeed Jesus came to liberate the oppressed. That was the message of Black Power. Jesus and Black Power were advocating the same thing. If we didn't think Black Power was Christian it was because we had accepted an interpretation of Christianity derived from the culture of white supremacy. When theologians and churches interpret and preach the gospel in a way that ignores society's systematic denial of a people's humanity, as in slavery, Jim Crow segregation, and lynching, their gospel and theology are antithetical to the message of Jesus Christ.

Black Theology and Black Power saved my life as a theologian, allowing me to fulfill the true purpose of my calling. I had heard many ministers talk and preach about when God called them into the ministry. Some said they heard a loud voice, which said, "Go preach!" and they stopped what they were doing and heeded the call. Others said it was a "still small voice" they could barely hear, and from which they tried to run away. No minister told the story of his or her calling in the same way. I felt called and entered the ministry at sixteen during my first semester of college, and preached my first sermon on December 12, 1954, in my brother's church, Spring Hill AME. There was a deep feeling inside me, pushing me to bear witness to what was right and true, and I did my best to "preach it" that Sunday morning. I told the story of Jesus doing good, healing the sick and giving sight to the blind. I was limited in what I knew about the gospel. But I felt its liberating truth, and I was committed to interpreting it in its deepest spiritual and intellectual dimensions.

Soon I realized, though, that I could not serve as a pastor under AME bishops, who had no genuine system of accountability. Their demeaning disrespect for pastors reminded me of arbitrary white authority; the only difference was color. I went to seminary knowing I couldn't pastor an AME church, and had no intention of serving as one in another denomination. Yet I didn't go to seminary with the idea of pursuing a Ph.D. It was far from my mind until William Hordern convinced me that I could and should get a doctorate in theology.

When I graduated from Garrett, college teaching was my highest aspiration. It was a job I loved, but it didn't feel like I was fulfilling the calling that had sent me into the ministry. A chance encounter in 1965 with Dr. Benjamin E. Mays, the great scholar of black religion and legendary president of Morehouse College, started me thinking about teaching *and* scholarship as ministry. He also had taught and inspired Martin Luther King Jr. and was the joint author (with J. W. Nicholson) of *The Black Church* (1933) and the sole author of the classic *The Negro's God* (1938). When I was a speaker at Morris Brown College, an AME institution in Atlanta and a participant in the Atlanta University Center, Dr. Mays invited me to have breakfast with him and his wife. I was shocked because I had never met him and didn't know that he was aware of me.

I was very nervous as I walked over that morning to his house to meet him, wondering anxiously why he invited me to breakfast. I was not important, just a beginning teacher of religion and philosophy at Philander Smith College. When I rang the doorbell, Dr. Mays opened the door, warmly greeted me, and invited me to join him and his wife for breakfast. I have no memory of what was served or who served it. I was in a trance and only vaguely remember that we were sitting on a sun porch in the bright sunlight. What followed that day so transformed my thinking about myself that it is difficult to this day to recall exactly what happened. I was so nervous that I hardly said more than five or six sentences during the whole time. I listened in awe. It is difficult to describe what it meant to be in the presence of such an outstanding intellectual, one so deeply committed to the black freedom movement. I just tried to keep from shaking.

Dr. Mays did nearly all the talking, telling me about the quality of my mind and that I had an important future as a scholar. It was similar to what William Hordern had told me when he encouraged me about my academic ability to get a doctorate. Dr. Mays was telling me about my potential to become a first-rate scholar even before I had published anything. How could he know what potential I had? Had he attended one of my lectures? I was so awed that I couldn't ask anything like that. He saw more possibility in me than I recognized in myself. His words started me thinking in a new way about my intellectual potential and calling to ministry.

I went back to Philander, and left to teach at Adrian, and now some years later I was sitting in my brother's church office, writing my reflections on the gospel and blackness, trying to fulfill the promise Dr. Mays saw in me. It was amazing. I had to pinch myself to see if it was really happening or just merely a dream.

I would walk around in the office of my brother's church, reading aloud what I had written, amazed at the clarity and power of the message and the beauty of the words coming out of me. I felt as though it wasn't me writing, but some spiritual force telling me what to write. I felt as if black folk in Bearden were talking to me, telling me to speak the truth, saying "Amen" and "Hallelujah" at the end of many sentences the way they responded to preachers who charismatically spoke the truth they felt. I even felt the spirits of my slave ancestors rising up inside me, whispering words of encouragement, telling me to be strong in black faith and not to be afraid as long as I knew I was writing God's truth and not seeking to satisfy my ego. I knew my book, if published, was going to make a lot of people angry. But I didn't care. When I thought about all the suffering that black people went through, from the slave ships to the lynching trees, I just couldn't be bothered by whether others—especially white people—would be offended by what I was writing.

Many people (especially my colleagues at Adrian) didn't always understand me. They thought I was just a contrary Negro, difficult and angry, as if I had no reason to be that way. But I was obsessed with what I was writing. God created Negroes black, which must be good. White people defamed blackness, and that's evil. Jesus came to liberate blackness from whiteness. To ask me to back away from blackness would be like asking Malcolm to stop talking about it or Martin to shut up about poverty, racism, and the war in Vietnam or James Baldwin to stop bearing witness to the power of love. In different ways they paid a high price—in the case of Malcolm and Martin, with their lives. The price I would pay—mostly loneliness as a theologian—would be small by comparison.

To write well I had to reflect the black experience in my writing. Love of black people enabled me to find the language, the words needed to say what had to be said so black people would recognize that I was one of their own, doing theology in a style that reflected their experience. I didn't discard European theology and philosophy—I continue to read

it today—but black theology began with deconstruction—
that is, *dismantling* the oppressive, white theologies I was
taught in graduate school, theologies that not only ignored
black people but blinded me to the rich treasure in the black
religious tradition. Using Barth, Tillich, Niebuhr, as my
theological authorities would never liberate my mind and
black people from white supremacy. Their theologies were
not created to free me to think independently and to liberate
black people. They were created to keep white people free
and blacks enslaved. I had to deconstruct white theologies to
destroy their effects on my mind so that I would be opened
to listen to the black voices from slavery, emerging from the
ashes of the black holocaust. I had to look back and *recover*
the black heritage that gave birth to me.

I had heard stories of Richard Allen and Absalom Jones
who, along with other blacks, walked out of St. George
Methodist Episcopal Church in Philadelphia in the late eighteenth century, inspiring Allen to organize an independent
African church called Bethel. Other African churches were
organized under similar circumstances, and they joined
with Allen, eventually founding the African Methodist
Episcopal Church in 1816. Their walk out of St. George was
an exodus, somewhat like the ancient Israelites from Egypt.
Their creation of the AME Church denomination was their
covenant with God, like Israel at Sinai. Richard Allen was
their Moses. I knew also about other Methodist and Baptist
churches where blacks walked out like Allen, and they too
founded church denominations—primarily because whites
refused to treat blacks with respect.

I began to learn about other great prophets, like the black
Presbyterian minister Henry Highland Garnet, who, in an

address to slaves, urged them to resist, saying, "If hereditary bondsmen would be free, they must themselves strike the blow." Garnet remained a revolutionary voice within the white Presbyterian Church. I was greatly moved to read these words and to learn of Nathaniel Paul, a Baptist minister of Albany, New York, who questioned God's passivity in the face of slavery, like an "unconcerned spectator" when "thine own creatures" were "reduced to a state of mere vassalage and misery." These radical statements by black ministers inspired me to stand on their shoulders. Even Daniel A. Payne, who was elected an AME Bishop (1852), questioned the existence of God and asked, "If he did exist, is he just? If so, why does he suffer one race to oppress and enslave another . . . ?"

I was discovering among such black voices the material to create a black theology. Although the black denominational churches did not oppose slavery, lynching, and Jim Crow segregation with the revolutionary spirit I believed was demanded by the gospel, nonetheless there was always a remnant in the black religious tradition to which a theologian could appeal. Among that remnant was the Reverend Henry McNeal Turner, who in 1898 proclaimed that "God is a Negro," an important resource for my development of black theology. The rise of the civil rights movement came out of the black church and became a profound expression of its true meaning. While Black Power is not the church, it is a profound expression of blackness that all black people are called to embrace. All this deconstruction and recovery prepared me for the task of construction: the making of a black theology defined by black suffering and struggle.

I would never have been able to write *Black Theology and*

Black Power without going back home to my people. My brother's church was the right place for me to write because the Black Spirit was in the air, all around me, grounding me theologically as I wrote, thinking about my ancestors who refused to believe that God created them to be slaves or second-class citizens.

After four or five weeks, writing about a chapter a week, I thought I was finished. I was exhausted, but hopeful. I carried my writing around for about two months, never letting it out of my sight for long, reading it over again and again, editing for more clarity and power, wondering whether I had written anything worthwhile, doubting that what I had written was worthy of the past three and a half centuries of black suffering.

On my drive back from Little Rock to Adrian, I paid a visit to Charles H. Long, a well-known Negro professor of history of religions at the University of Chicago and a native of Little Rock, Arkansas. I didn't know him well, but he was gracious enough to welcome me into his home for a meal and a conversation about my book.

Even though he hadn't read my manuscript and in fact didn't show any interest in reading it, Long encouraged me to submit it for publication. I didn't know what to think about our strange encounter. I was twelve years his junior and literally afraid of his intellectual power, which was well known in academic circles, especially the American Academy of Religion, where he was one of the first blacks to serve as president. He was also an editor of the well-known *History of Religions* journal, along with the great Mircea Eliade and Joseph Kitagawa. Long's intellectual acumen would be on prominent display among black religion scholars in the Society for the Study of Black Religion soon after my book was published. In time he would become my fiercest critic. But even then, as we talked about my manuscript in Chicago, I sensed a conflict brewing. I didn't know quite what to make of it, but I sensed it reflected the long-standing tension between theology and history of religions. I could tell by his sly look that he had something up his sleeve. He was cagey but friendly; I sensed he was going to be a thorn in my side, though I would never be able to figure out why.

Back in Adrian, I gave my manuscript to Lester Scherer to read. He provided many helpful editorial suggestions, making it clearer and more persuasive. He never tried to soften anything. Then I decided to send my manuscript off to C. Eric Lincoln, to get his opinion of it, since he had published an edited version of my first essay in his book, *Is Anybody Listening to Black America?* (1968). Within a week he called me and told me with much excitement that I had written a significant book and asked whether he could arrange for it to be published. "Yes!" I responded, with great joy, excitement, and surprise. Then he said, "It needs two more chapters. You've got to say more about black theology." "That is for my next book," I replied. "No, you need to give an anticipation of it in this one."

I did as Lincoln instructed, and wrote two more chapters, focusing on "Some Perspectives of Black Theology" (chapter 5) and "Revolution, Violence, and Reconciliation in Black Theology" (chapter 6). To my great surprise, those chapters flowed out of me much more easily than the first four. They were the beginning of my *constructive* theological reflection on black theology. Both chapters were written in about two weeks. I was teaching all day and writing and editing nearly all night, listening to the blues in my "Blue Room."

In the earlier chapters, I was analyzing several subjects: black power, the gospel of Jesus, and white and black churches. Black Power was defined as the political liberation of black people by any means necessary. The gospel of Jesus was defined as God's coming reign in the life, teachings, and death of Jesus, liberating the poor into a new realm of existence. Jesus's liberation was both political and spiritual, fighting the Roman Empire and giving those who believe and follow him a salvation that no one could take away. White and black churches had failed to preach and live Jesus's gospel of liberation. They were too concerned about their own survival as institutions and failed to heed Jesus's saying: "For those who want to save their life will lose it, and those who lose their life for my sake and for the sake of the gospel, will save it" (Mark 8:35). My theological perspective was buried in the analysis. But in the chapters on black theology, I was taking a risk and a much more radical and constructive stand, and I was prepared to defend it against whoever would challenge me. The black poet LeRoi Jones (Amiri Baraka) defined the Black Spirit that would be my guide.

Show the chains. Let them see the chains as object and subject, and let them see the chains fall away.[1]

The ideas advanced in those two chapters on black theology have remained with me to this day—after nearly fifty

1. LeRoi Jones (Amiri Baraka), "What the Arts Need Now," *Negro Digest* 16, no. 6 (April 1967): 5.

years of writing. Ideas derived from books change, depending on what's in vogue. As Albert Camus said, "I have never seen anyone die for the ontological argument. . . . The meaning of life is the most urgent of questions."[2] I was searching for the meaning of black life in America from a black theological perspective. First, I had to deconstruct white theology and white and black churches before I could construct a black theology. Black theology's starting point was black suffering, the black condition, because there is where the Christ event is, God's revelation in black pain, black agony. Black suffering, then, is the ultimate religious authority, the final authority on all theological statements.

With verve and a determined theological will, I proceeded to address controversial topics in theology, the churches, and society, including revolution, violence, and reconciliation. What I said about these ideas would become the most controversial themes in black theology. Blackness was my authority, my starting point. I quoted the black cultural nationalist Maulana Karenga: "The fact that I am Black is my ultimate reality."[3] White and black religion scholars could not believe that a Christian theologian would say something like that. That was because they had made Christianity *white*, completely identified with European and white American culture. Jesus was not white. "Christ is black, baby,"[4] I proclaimed. That's the only way we can understand Christ in a culture defined by white supremacy.

---

2. Albert Camus, *The Myth of Sisyphus and Other Essays*, trans. Justin O'Brien (New York: Vintage Books, 1955), 3, 4.

3. Cited in Cone, *Black Theology and Black Power* (Maryknoll, NY: Orbis Books, 1997), 34.

4. Ibid., 68.

The Black Christ is the liberating spirit in the black revolution as defined by Black Power. Violence is not black people's primary response to white supremacy, but self-defense is important for black dignity. The ever-present violence of white supremacy—psychic, physical, and spiritual—in the black community should be the chief concern of white Americans. Reconciliation is a white responsibility.

Whites didn't like the words "Black Power" and "black theology." I couldn't care less about what they liked or didn't. As Carmichael said: "For once black people are going to use the words they want to use—not just the words whites want to hear."[5] I wasn't writing to please whites. I was writing to empower the wounded spirits of blacks who were trying to stay in the church and also struggle for justice as they embraced their blackness in America. I also wrote to encourage whites to become black. "God's Word of reconciliation means we can only be justified by becoming black."

"How can I, a *white* [person] become black?" was the most frequent question whites asked me. "Being black in America has very little to do with skin color," I wrote. "To be black means that your heart, your soul, your mind, and your body are where the dispossessed are."[6] To become black is like what Jesus told Nicodemus, that he must be "born again," that is, "born of water and Spirit" (John 3), the Black Spirit of liberation.

Black religion scholars would push back hard on this theological claim. Among my fiercest critics, and at the same

---

5. Clayborne Carson, *In Struggle: SNCC and the Black Awakening of the 1960s* (Cambridge, MA: Harvard University Press, 1981), 219.

6. *Black Theology and Black Power*, 151.

time a devoted friend, was Gayraud Wilmore, author of the important text *Black Religion and Black Radicalism* (1973). But I held firm to my claim, despite his objections, because I was speaking primarily symbolically, while Wilmore was speaking primarily historically. History significantly informs what theologians say, but it's not the final arbiter in theological matters. The Word of God, Jesus the Christ, as revealed in scripture and black experience, is the final judge. I didn't see how anyone could be a Christian and not understand that.

When I finished *Black Theology and Black Power*, I could not believe what I had done—that I had written a book that spoke to my heart, soul, and mind—a book about to be published, so the world would know where I was coming from. The working title for my book was *Christianity and Black Power*, but the additional two chapters put black theology at the center of my perspective. Seabury Press had accepted my book for publication. My editor, Arthur Buckley, was thrilled with the two additional chapters and suggested the title *Black Theology and Black Power*. "'Black theology' should come first in the title because that's who you are," he said. "Black Power should be second, because it is the spirit behind black theology. Eliminate 'Christianity' from the title because its meaning has been corrupted by white supremacy." I liked what he was saying and didn't need to be convinced. I was a theologian through and through. I had no desire to be a Black Power advocate like Stokely Carmichael. For me, Black Power merely pointed to the much larger theme of liberation, which my next book would explicate.

In December, I gave four lectures at Colgate taken from *Black Theology and Black Power*. Debates among the faculty and students—both black and white—were intense, questioning the very idea of a black theology and whether it could be reconciled with the universalism of the Christian gospel. "There is no universalism in the gospel that is not at the same time particular," I asserted with emphasis. "This is precisely what the incarnation means, God becoming human in Jesus." God comes to us in the particular, which points us to the universal. God is talking to us in Black Power, in blackness. Just as the Romans crucified Jesus in the first century, white people are lynching black people today.

"What about the violence in Black Power?," they asked, "How can it be reconciled with Jesus's emphasis on love?" "Black Power is a response to the violence of white supremacy," I retorted, "and I notice you are silent about white violence against blacks, which is the main problem of violence in the United States. Black theology and Black Power don't advocate violence, but they do advocate the right of blacks to defend their humanity by any means necessary." Malcolm's phrase "by any means necessary" touched off a firestorm in the school, with some whites saying I was advocating violence. I wasn't, but straight talking by a black person could create alarm among whites. I didn't allow their insecurity to throw me off my focus. I talked with self-confidence about scripture and the Western theological tradition from Athanasius, Augustine, Luther, and Calvin to Barth, Tillich, and Niebuhr. It was an amazing experience for me to argue toe-to-toe with white theologians on their academic turf, but I actually enjoyed the combat. Black students seemed proud of my performance, and they accompanied me everywhere I went.

The president, Gene Bartlett, offered me a position on Colgate's faculty as associate professor of theology. I told him I needed to think carefully about where my next move should be, since other schools were expressing interest in my work. It was thrilling to talk theology at a high intellectual level and feel that I was in my comfort zone. But an intellectual challenge was not my only interest. My primary interest was to move out of Adrian to a place where I would be near a thriving black community that was religiously alive and engaged in cultural production, historical writing, and political empowerment.

I had no way of knowing whether my book would make an impact on theology and churches in the United States. But I was hopeful. My editor was excited and Lincoln was, too. Yet, I had to walk this strange journey alone because there was no one to walk with me. It was lonely; there was no black theologian I could talk to about what I was trying to do. I didn't care that white theologians would say it was too influenced by the times—Black Power and other political and cultural movements. What Nina Simone said about an artist expressed my feelings about a theologian: "How can you be an artist and not reflect the times? That to me is the definition of an artist."[7] A theologian too!

---

7. Cited in Salamishah Tillet's review of the documentary film "What Happened, Miss Simone?," *New York Times,* Sunday, Arts and Leisure, June 21, 2015, 1, 10.

CHAPTER 3

You Oughta Been There

A Black Theology of Liberation

"You don't mean that, do you?" asked John Bennett, the president of Union Theological Seminary, as we sat in his office, about a month after I had begun teaching there. A statement in my first book, widely reported in the media, had been called to his attention by several professors and students in the seminary community. He was referring to my claim that "the white church is the Antichrist."

"That's hyperbole, isn't it?" he asked, anxiously.

"Absolutely not!" I replied firmly. "I mean it literally—every word of it."

I spoke in a direct manner, looking him in the eye with no concern about protecting my job. Though he seemed shocked, I was going to say it, as long as it was the truth. I had no further intention of wearing a mask.

By this time *Black Theology and Black Power* had been out for several months. I knew Bennett had read it; he had also sent it to his friend Reinhold Niebuhr, now in retirement from Union, but regarded by many as the most important

American theologian of the twentieth century. Assuming that the renowned social ethicist would reject my book as too militant, Bennett had worried that Niebuhr would voice concerns about my appointment to the faculty at Union. In a letter to Niebuhr, Bennett had written, "I am sending you a copy of a book by our new Assistant Professor of Theology, James Cone, on *Black Theology and Black Power*. I am sure that you will find this book in many ways difficult to take."[1] But Bennett had misjudged Niebuhr. His own critique of liberalism was quite similar to the arguments I was making against white supremacy. As far back as the 1920s, he had shaken up American Protestant liberalism, charging it with lacking "the spirit of enthusiasm not to say fanaticism, which is so necessary to move the world out of its beaten tracks. It is too intellectual and too little emotional to be an efficient force in history."[2]

In an immediate reply, Niebuhr wrote, "I hope your warning about me not liking the book may prove to be in error."[3] And so it was. After reading it, Niebuhr responded to Bennett, "Thank you for sending Professor Cone's *Black Theology and Black Power*. I was tremendously interested in the book, and am not as critical as you anticipated that I would be. After all, the Negroes are the most genuine proletarians that we have in our middle class culture, and there is bound to be resentment

---

1. Bennett's letter to Niebuhr, June 16, 1969.

2. Reinhold Niebuhr, "The Twilight of Liberalism," *The New Republic*, June 14, 1919; idem, "The Confessions of a Tired Radical," *The Christian Century*, August 30, 1928; Reinhold Niebuhr, "Let the Liberal Churches Stop Fooling Themselves!" *The Christian Century*, March 25, 1931.

3. Niebuhr's letter to Bennett, June 18, 1969.

in our Negro minority which he expresses adequately. . . . I think he will be an excellent man on your faculty."[4]

What Niebuhr could see, and what Bennett couldn't, was what he called in *Moral Man and Immoral Society* "a sublime madness in the soul." "Rationality," he wrote, "belongs to the cool observers"—a term that aptly described Bennett's response to black theology. On the other hand, he wrote, "The absolutist and fanatic are dangerous, but they are also necessary."[5] I had read Niebuhr's *Moral Man* in seminary and again as I was writing my book. I had resonated with his words: "The oppressed . . . have a higher moral right to challenge their oppressors than these have to maintain their rule by force."[6]

Bennett shared this correspondence with me. Frankly, Niebuhr's response didn't surprise me. He recognized that my work was not a careless outburst but a cogent and passionate argument. What did surprise me was to discover how shocked Bennett seemed to be with the radical nature of my language; it was, after all, entirely consistent with that of his longtime friend and colleague. Nevertheless, I wasn't really interested in Niebuhr's thoughts about black theology, any more than Bennett's. No white man could instruct me on this subject. And so, when President Bennett asked me whether I was being "hyperbolic" in naming the white church as the Antichrist, I responded without flinching.

"White supremacy," I said, "is the Antichrist in America because it has killed and crippled tens of millions of black

---

4. Niebuhr to Bennett, June 29, 1969.
5. Reinhold Niebuhr, *Moral Man and Immoral Society* (New York: Charles Scribner's Sons, 1932), 277, 221, 222.
6. Ibid., 234.

bodies and minds in the modern world. It has also committed genocide against the indigenous people of this land. If that isn't demonic, I don't know what is. White supremacy is America's original sin. It is found in every aspect of American life, especially churches, seminaries, and theology."

"If you think white seminaries and churches are the Antichrist," he asked, "why are you teaching at Union?"

"My father," I said, "who just died of heart failure, probably from the stress of white supremacy, cut wood, billets and logs to support his family; I work at Union. I see no difference. We have both had to deal with the stress of white supremacy every day. And as long as I don't burn Union down, I might as well work here. It is as simple as that, like working at Macy's department store."

That was the spirit of blackness speaking. I could see that President Bennett was visibly upset, perhaps wondering why he and the faculty had appointed me. Clearly, no other black person had ever spoken to him in such emotionally charged terms, and it made him nervous.

I later learned that Bennett asked C. Eric Lincoln to have a talk with me and get me to tone down my militancy. To his credit, Lincoln declined. He was born and reared in Alabama and knew well the violence of white supremacy. I felt that I was articulating a militancy he shared but did not express outwardly. In fact, it was Lincoln who was chiefly responsible for my ending up at Union, just as it was he who was responsible for putting my first book into the hands of a publisher. He probably didn't know what he was getting himself into, and neither did I. Things seemed to happen, without leaving time for me to think about whether I could do it. Before I could exhale from writing my first book, Lincoln called and dropped two bombshells that left me temporarily disoriented.

"You should teach at Union," he said. He was talking about the leading seminary in the world, the place where Reinhold Niebuhr and Paul Tillich had taught and become famous—and where, I might add, Lincoln had been appointed as its first black professor, two years before I arrived in 1969.[7] I was truly shocked by his idea. Teaching at Colgate Rochester Divinity School was one thing, but Union was on another planet.

"From Adrian College to Union Seminary! You must be crazy," I told him.

"You can do it," Lincoln declared. "Trust me," he said. "One more thing," he added. "I am editing a book series on black religion, and I want you to write the first volume for it."

"What!" I reacted, shocked at the thought of writing another book so soon after the first. "I just finished a book!"

"I know," he said. "And it's a damn good one. But you must not be contented with one book. You have many books in you. You have much to say, and only you can say it the way you say it. There is no theological voice like yours. The black community needs you and white people do too. The theological world needs you."

"When do you want it?" I asked.

"In September," he said.

"That's only nine months from now," I shouted. "It's impossible!"

---

7. Laurence N. Jones preceded Lincoln a few years earlier as dean of students and became a professor of Afro-American church history in 1970.

"You can do it," he said confidently. I was amazed at the trust he expressed in me.

"Well, if you think I can, I'll do my best." Those were my last words on the subject.

I knew I had another book in me. *Black Theology and Black Power* was only a beginning. But did I have the resources and talent to write another one? Nevertheless, the fire was still burning in my bones, and I had no choice but to stoke it. I had to keep writing. After all, I was the *only* black systematic theologian in the United States writing about black people, and it weighed on my shoulders. The black revolution that was exploding all over America needed a systematic theology. If I didn't do it, who would? "Am I going to let my people down when they are dying in the streets?" I asked myself. I couldn't do that! Another installment on my debt was due. I had to do my part for the black freedom struggle. No excuses! "Now is the time," as Martin King had often said.

I decided to accept Lincoln's challenge, knowing that it would expose me to a cavalcade of criticism—some of which I had already experienced. When I had shared my book and my earlier essay on "Christianity and Black Power" with my former doctoral advisor, Philip S. Watson, he had written me an angry letter: "All you have done is try to justify black people killing me and other whites," he said—an absurd statement to which I could not respond. I wasn't advocating violence against white people. I was exposing and declaring my fierce opposition to white violence against black people. I was trying to speak the same truth that sent Jesus to the cross. I couldn't back away from the truth I saw in Jesus's life and death. I was prepared to discuss its theological merits, but I couldn't compromise it or allow it to be twisted into "black racism," as Watson and other white theologians tried to label it.

To keep my composure in the face of such criticism, I thought about Malcolm X, who only finished the eighth grade but held his own at nearly every major university in the United States, speaking three times at Harvard, as well as at Princeton, Yale, Berkeley, and even Oxford University. James Baldwin had only a high school education, but he told the truth about America and race with an eloquence that stunned the world. Although Martin King earned a doctorate in systematic theology from Boston University, it was the black church experience that prepared him for the great spiritual and political challenges he faced in the black freedom movement. What did Malcolm X, Martin King, and James Baldwin have that enabled them to speak the truth with spiritual, artistic, and political power? It was more than intellectual talent. Many people were smart, but most of them made no difference in the fight for racial justice. Martin, Malcolm, and Jimmy had the courage of their convictions. I had to find a similar courage.

My father, Charlie Cone, had that kind of courage. Despite the threats of lynching, he stood up to the white school board in Bearden, and declared the obvious: that white and Negro schools were not equal. He then filed a lawsuit against the school board and refused to back down, even as other Negro men withdrew their names. If I had the courage to continue my attack against racism in white theology, it had come from my father. My mother, Lucy, had the gift of speech, and she often helped Charlie find the words he needed to speak effectively. I admired my parents more than anyone. They were the role models that shaped my life. If Charlie Cone could do it, with only a sixth-grade education, and Lucy could say it with only a ninth, so could I, because I came from them. They produced me. Their blood ran through my veins. Charlie gave me courage, and Lucy gave me language. I needed both to express what was burning in my soul.

But could I write a systematic theology with the fire, clarity, power, and beauty that would make people want to read what I wrote? My parents were not writers, and systematic theology, as defined by Europeans, could be a boring subject, largely limited to academic conversations among professors and their graduate students. I had written a dissertation on Karl Barth's *Church Dogmatics*, and it would be hard to find anything more boring than that, especially in relation to black people's freedom struggle. The fire burning in me could not be expressed in the style of Barth's *Church Dogmatics* or Paul Tillich's *Systematic Theology*. I had to write in a *new* theological language from the underside of American history—the language of the black sermon and song, and in the spirit of the great preachers and singers I had heard all over Arkansas and in Chicago and Detroit. I did not want to write anything that black people would not understand and read and hear as their own experience. If I couldn't preach it, I wouldn't write it.

Yet, while I wanted to write a systematic theology *for* black people, I also wanted to deepen my dialogue with white theologians about the truth of race in America, and show that their failure to address white supremacy was supporting racism. I didn't want to get sidetracked into theological and philosophical abstractions. I wanted black people to know what I was saying about whiteness and Christianity. And I wanted white theologians to know it was time for them to face their own racism. I accepted the task of speaking to whites in black language and in the discipline of systematic theology, which few African Americans knew anything about.

Systematic theology is a specialized and challenging discipline, and an excellent tool for interpreting the Christian gospel. If preachers don't know what the gospel means for their time and place, they can't preach it. Black churches suffer greatly because they have not been as concerned about training theologians as preachers. Churches need preachers to proclaim the gospel. But they also need theologians to interpret it. Without disciplined interpretation, preachers would proclaim the same prepackaged message that previous generations handed down to them. Reflecting on theology keeps preachers up to date, enabling them to take an ancient gospel text and make it read like the front page of the *New York Times*.

Theologians use many resources to interpret the gospel, including the Bible, the writings of other theologians from the past, as well as philosophy, sociology, history, and the current worldviews of their time. What they don't usually acknowledge is that they also bring their own experience and biases. None of us is free of bias, and the more power a group has, the more distorted its views. How could white theologians interpret the gospel without a bias toward white supremacy? They couldn't, unless they turned away from their dominant culture and religion and toward the culture and religion of the powerless. "I thank you, Father," Jesus said, ". . . because you have hidden these things from the wise and the intelligent and have revealed them to infants"

(Matt 11:25). When that theological insight became clear to me, I was ready to write.

The fundamental problem that troubled me was the relation between the gospel of Jesus and the reality of black suffering and black resistance, as defined by the civil rights and Black Power movements. I wanted to construct a black theology—a theology that would be *black* like Malcolm and *Christian* like Martin. What did the Christian gospel mean in the political context of the Negro struggle for justice (Martin) and the cultural fight for black dignity and self-respect (Malcolm)? That was the central question as I wrote *Black Theology and Black Power*. But in my next book I wanted to go deeper into the meaning of *liberation* and *blackness*.

Although Malcolm X said that "Christianity is the white man's religion," Martin King placed it at the center of his ministry in church and society. Both inspired me; but who was right, Martin or Malcolm? Civil rights or Black Power? Integration or separation? If I were going remain a *Christian* like Martin, that identity would have to be rooted in being *black* like Malcolm, because, as Malcolm said, "we are black first and everything else second." I was black before I was a Christian. Martin and Malcolm, therefore, had to go together, which meant being unashamedly black and unapologetically Christian.

James Baldwin, a former Harlem storefront preacher, said, "It took many years of vomiting up all the filth I had been taught about myself and half-believed, before I was able to walk on the earth as though I had a right to be here."[8] Unlike

---

8. James Baldwin, "They Can't Turn Back," in *Collected Essays*, ed. Toni Morrison (New York: Library of America, 1998), 636.

Baldwin, I have always felt that I had a right to be here and never believed, even for a moment, what white people said about me. I never thought I was inferior to anybody. I knew my mother and father loved me, as did the people of Macedonia AME Church. At home and in church, I encountered God's love, revealed in Jesus, the man from Nazareth, crucified in Jerusalem. Yet there was not a deep and explicit affirmation of blackness at home or in church. We were proud Negroes but didn't know anything about Black Nationalism, the Nation of Islam, Marcus Garvey, or the great black intellectual W. E. B. Du Bois. On the contrary, the white Jesus was everywhere: in pictures, on church fans, Sunday school literature, and stained-glass windows. "Wash me," the congregation at Macedonia cried out to God, "and I shall be whiter than snow."

I wrote *Black Theology and Black Power* as an attack on racism in white churches and an attack on self-loathing in black churches. I was not interested in making an academic point about theology; rather, I was issuing a manifesto *against* whiteness and *for* blackness in an effort to liberate Christians from white supremacy.

In my next book, *A Black Theology of Liberation*, I also wanted to address white theology and seminaries. Nevertheless, I found it exceedingly difficult to discard the assumptions about theology that I was taught in graduate school. White teachers introduced me to theology, told me what it was, and who the great theologians were. They told me to read their books and to write about them; they told me when I interpreted them correctly and when I didn't. And then they decided whether I knew European theologians well enough and could write about them with enough intellectual sophistication to pass their courses and go on to doctoral studies. If I were successful in writing well about the Western theological tradition, I would be given a doctoral degree and recommended for a faculty position. I got my Ph.D. in systematic theology and left to teach European theology to black students at Philander Smith College in Little Rock, Arkansas, who had little interest in what was clearly irrelevant to their daily lives in the land of Jim Crow. Then I went to teach white students at Adrian College in Michigan who had even less interest in Bultmann, Barth, and Tillich.

It was not easy to break loose from the white theological straitjacket. If I had thought about it too long, I wouldn't have written anything. It was Malcolm's spirit of blackness that shook me up, turned me around, stirred my soul, stimulated my spiritual imagination, and reminded me to think for myself and for the people who raised and nurtured me to adulthood. I soaked myself in blackness, embraced it as my birthright, and let blackness recreate me into someone my professors would not recognize. Blackness gave me the insight and power to write *A Black Theology of Liberation* with reckless abandon.

Yet to write a black liberation theology for the black freedom movement I had to liberate myself from what I'd learned in seminary studying systematic theology. How could I write about black liberation while remaining enslaved to the methodology and ideas of white European theologians? "A strong spirit transcends rules," proclaimed the great musician Prince,[9] who left a treasure of music that expressed his

---

9. See Jon Pareles, "A Mesmerizing Master of Pop," *New York Times*, April 22, 2016, B10.

wild, free spirit. No theology of dead or living white men could control the spirit of blackness. Black liberation theology was "born free," free to say what the spirit says, what the black experience demands, as it wrestles with pain and suffering, joy and triumph. When I listened to and observed black musicians, singing and playing their instruments, bodies moving and swaying, they inspired me to write systematic theology the way they sang and played, the way black bodies moved, getting funky, "like funk is going out of style." I listened to their cadence, beat, sound, and tone, and then tried to capture what they did in words. European theologians were too rational and abstract to understand what was happening in the black experience. They knew nothing about funk.

In *A Black Theology of Liberation*, I tried to capture the funk of black people as they expressed it, using a Malcolm X improvisational, militant style, a "don't mess with me" attitude. So I didn't care what white theologians thought about black liberation theology. They didn't give a damn about black people. We were invisible in their writings, not even worthy of mention. Why should I care about what they thought? Intentionally I tried to disrupt the ways they did systematic theology, using sources and norms they created and repeated throughout history while at the same time enslaving and segregating blacks at will. It gave me great pleasure to see their anger as I brazenly broke every theological rule they created—like a blues or jazz artist improvising and permutating, doing his or her thing. That was the Malcolm X part of black liberation theology breaking loose in me—what the black people in Bearden called "showing out," "getting beside himself," "acting mannish."

I couldn't write like Baldwin or speak like Martin or Malcolm, but I could write black liberation theology like James Cone. Hopefully, I could inspire black people to reject the religion of white supremacy, which is camouflaged by white theology and worshiped in rich white churches. I drew on a black cultural aesthetic, the artistic excellence in the "dynamite voices" of black poets and playwrights, who asked "a revolutionary question":

> must I shoot the
> white man dead
> to free the nigger
> in his head? [10]

Black liberation theology came out of black culture and religion, and it celebrated a new freedom to talk about God and Jesus in a jazz mode, a blues style, and with the sound of the spirituals. That was where its mojo came from—its magic. I was more concerned about remaining true to black magic than creating new theological ideas that would impress white theologians but would put ordinary blacks to sleep. I wanted to wake up black people and let them know that the day of the white Christ was over. A new Black Messiah was in town.

Chinua Achebe, the great African writer, author of the classic novel *Things Fall Apart* (1958), said, "Art cannot be on the side of the oppressor." He continued: "A poet cannot be a slave trader."[11] I didn't know much about art, but I did

---

10. See Conrad Kent Rivers, "Watts," cited in Don L. Lee (Haki R. Madhubuti), *Dynamite Voices: Black Poets of the 1960s* (Detroit: Broadside Press, 1971), 38.

11. See Dorothy Randall-Tsuruta, "In Dialogue to Define Aesthetics: James Baldwin and Chinua Achebe" (1981), in James Baldwin,

know that a Christian theologian couldn't be on the side of the oppressor, as a slave trader or a slaveholder. Christian theology is for the liberation of all humanity, and it could never be neutral in the fight against oppression. That much I knew. And that was how *A Black Theology of Liberation* was born: with the spirit of Martin and Malcolm, Jimmy, and the black poets of the 1960s.

I did not talk with any black religion scholars about what I was doing. I didn't know any of them, except C. Eric Lincoln, and he was a sociologist and offered no advice. I was acquainted with Charles Long but he was a historian of religion and uninterested in what I was writing. I was on my own. But I thought then, as I do now, that no one could have influenced in any way the spirit in which I wrote. A force was driving me, bigger than myself.

This Black Spirit crying out in me, crying for freedom, was more important than any rational argument that could justify black liberation theology. I wrote most of *A Black Theology of Liberation* while I was teaching twelve hours a week at Adrian College. After teaching and counseling students most of the day, I went home to write in my blue room in the basement, with the blues and the spirituals and some jazz often playing quietly in the background as I reached down in the depths of my being for the spirit of blackness. It felt good, as the words flowed out of me. I was alone with my music, jamming, playing with words, expressing myself freely on paper as jazz musicians do on piano, saxophone, and drums. I could almost hear myself writing, as the words danced on paper, talking back to me. What I was writing was

Conversations with James Baldwin, ed. Fred L. Standley and Louis H. Pratt (Jackson: University Press of Mississippi, 1989), 211.

amazing to me, and I was not always sure where the words were coming from. They had a freedom that transcended me. The first sentence I wrote startled me: "Christian theology is a theology of liberation."[12] No one had ever said that before. It became the core of my theology. I knew I was right because it felt true.

But just because a religious claim feels true doesn't mean it is true. What evidence could I advance to support the claim that Christian theology is defined by liberation? The black experience and scripture were my central sources for defining the meaning of Christian theology. Both were essential and could not be separated, but the black experience was the starting point. Yet when I examined both the black experience and scripture, it became crystal clear that liberation was at the heart of Christian theology. After all, the central themes of the exodus, the prophets, and Jesus of Nazareth defined both the black experience and scripture.

> When Israel was in Egypt's land,
> Let my people go;
> Oppressed so hard they could not stand,
> Let my people go;
> Go down, Moses, 'way down in Egypt's land;
> Tell ole Pharaoh
> Let my people go.

I have seen the affliction of my people who are in Egypt, and have heard their cry because of their taskmasters; I

---

12. See James H. Cone, *A Black Theology of Liberation*, Fortieth Anniversary Edition (Maryknoll, NY: Orbis Books, 2010), 1.

know their sufferings, and I have come to deliver them
out of the land of the Egyptians. . . . (Exod 3:7–8)

The exodus was a liberation event—the deliverance of
Israelite slaves out of Egypt and the deliverance of African
slaves in the United States. The prophets, with their emphasis on justice for the poor, were also central to black experience and scripture. No scripture verse was more commonly
cited in the black religious experience than Amos's "Let justice roll down like waters, and righteousness like an ever-
flowing stream" (5:24).

Jesus of Nazareth was the third and most important
theme, defining God's commitment to liberation of the poor.
He is the liberator whose life was shaped by God's coming
justice for all, especially the poor. "Blessed are you who are
poor, for yours is the kingdom of God" (Luke 5:20). Jesus
lived among the poor, and, like them, he died on the cross.

Exodus, prophets, and Jesus—these three—defined the
meaning of liberation in black theology. I never deviated from
that core insight. Such insights came to me as if revealed by
the spirits of my ancestors long dead but now coming alive
to haunt and torment the descendants of the whites who had
killed them. No one could know what it felt like to write *A
Black Theology of Liberation*. I was doing something no black
person had ever done, traveling a road no one had trod
before—writing a theology out of the black experience and
for black people. I knew it was going to be published because
Eric Lincoln had given me his assurance. "Write your heart
out, son," he had told me, "write what you want to write. I've
got your back." That is what I did. I held nothing back.

I drew on everything I had been taught in seminary:

Barth, Brunner, Niebuhr, Tillich, Bonhoeffer, Bultmann, most of the European giants in theology. But I twisted them and bent their language in every way to speak *my* truth, not theirs. I loved writing. It liberated me theologically. Although I do not dance or sing, yet I felt like I was dancing with my words and singing a powerful tune, and the rhythm was like none I had seen in theology. The meaning of liberation was in the black style in which I was writing. I wrote what I felt the way I felt it. This book didn't come from library research, even though I read voraciously as I wrote. It came from what I had lived in the black community—its religion, culture, and politics. It came from what blacks had to do to express their freedom while living daily under white supremacy. Black liberation theology is a witness to black religious resistance to white domination. All I knew was that I wasn't going to be controlled in my thinking by white theologians. I had to write a black liberation theology that kicked white ass.

Where then did the word and meaning of liberation come from? The working title for my second book was initially *A Black Theology of Revolution.* The phrase "black revolution," after all, was the central description of the 1960s black freedom struggle. Yet, as I sat down to write, I decided to replace that word; while reflecting on the exodus, the prophets, and Jesus, I found that liberation, more than revolution, best defined what I wanted to say. The exodus was a deliverance, a *liberation* of a people out of slavery, and liberation was what black people in the United States were fighting for.

"What do we want?" was a frequent question leaders in the civil rights movement asked their audiences, and the answer was "Freedom!" Freedom and liberation were used interchangeably in the civil rights movement, with the younger Black Power people preferring the term liberation. "The politics of liberation" was the subtitle of Stokely Carmichael's book on *Black Power*, and he gave several speeches called "Toward Black Liberation."[13] The young Black Power advocates had grown tired of the word freedom, since it did not have the spark and energy indicated by Black Power. But both words were found throughout black history, religion, and culture. They were found in our songs and sermons, our stories and sayings.

Freedom and liberation were often used in both a political and a religious sense, especially in black liberation theology. In the political sense, liberation meant deliverance from the chains of slavery, segregation, and all forms of social, political, and economic oppression. But there was a deeper meaning of liberation and freedom that no oppressor could take away. To be free means that no one could deprive you of your dignity, your right to be black and free, no matter what white people did to you. Then there was the transcendent freedom that slaves were singing about when they referred to heaven—that place in the religious imagination that the slave master couldn't control. I remember encountering that liberation at Macedonia AME Church as a child. Blacks preached and sang about it, prayed for it, and testified to it. That same freedom was present in the civil rights and Black Power movements, in Martin Luther King Jr. and Stokely Carmichael. That was the liberation I was writing about in *A Black Theology of Liberation*.

---

13. See Stokely Carmichael, "Toward Black Liberation," in LeRoi Jones and Larry Neal, eds., *Black Fire: An Anthology of Afro-American Writing* (New York: William Morrow, 1968), 119–22.

Events happened fast after *Black Theology and Black Power* was accepted for publication. The book contract came and then the galleys in November 1968. I had to fight back tears as I meditated on what I had written and why I wrote it. There was no one with whom I could really share my experience. I could talk with my wife, Rose, who typed my manuscript, and Lester Scherer, who edited it, but neither really understood or felt what was happening to me. It took me into a pit of loneliness that would remain throughout most of my professional life.

In December 1968 I received a call from John C. Bennett, the president of Union, inviting me to a conversation with the faculty about a teaching appointment in systematic theology and about my forthcoming book, which they had also read in galleys. I was surprised, shocked, thrilled, and scared—all at the same time. Union was the top seminary in the United States. I was excited about the opportunity to test my ideas in such a challenging environment. But I was also nervous about the intellectual giants I would face: Bennett himself, as well as John McQuarrie, Daniel Day Williams, Paul Lehmann, and Roger Shinn. The night before my interview in January 1969 I couldn't sleep at all.

The next day I found myself surrounded by these scholars in the president's apartment. As I looked around the room I realized I had read most of their books in seminary and taught them at Philander Smith and Adrian. I knew I did not know as much about European and American theology and philosophy as they did. But I knew enough, and far more than they did about the black experience out of which I was writing. They were the experts on Europe, and I was the expert on black America. The most important thing was my confidence about the arguments I was advancing about the meaning of the gospel of Jesus for today. I was ready for them.

Paul Lehmann, author of the influential text *Ethics in a Christian Context,* began the faculty discussion by asking me, "Why in the hell did you write that book—*Black Theology and Black Power*?" I liked the directness of his question.

"I wrote it because I had to," I shot back. "I had no other choice, as a theologian, but to write the truth of the gospel of Jesus for America. Jesus's gospel today is Black Power, that is, the proclamation of liberation of black people from white supremacy, 'by any means necessary,' to use the language of Malcolm X." As I continued, I became increasingly excited. "White American theologians have ignored the gospel of God's liberation of black people from white supremacy. They have been more concerned about the latest theological fad coming out of Europe than about black bodies hanging from lynching trees." (Eric Lincoln, who was present, was smiling as I spoke.)

The more I talked the more relaxed I became, gaining confidence in my theological stand. Even though Lehmann and his colleagues were taken aback by what I said and the passion with which I said it, they could not deny my truth. The silence of white theology about slavery, segregation, and lynching spoke loudly about its implicit heresy.

"Any message that is not related to the liberation of the poor in society is not Christ's message," I said. "Any theology that is indifferent to the theme of God's liberation of the poor is not Christian theology." That was my stand, and on that point I did not deviate. "Because American theology has ignored the black poor, and the poor generally, it is not Christian theology," I said. "Period!"

The fifteen Union faculty members in President Bennett's apartment grew steadily silent in the face of my assault on white theology. They agreed that the liberation theme was central in the Bible, but it was not the only one, and blacks were not the only people suffering. I agreed with the latter point, but more debate was needed about the former.

Nevertheless, that conversation at Union boosted my intellectual self-confidence and removed any mystique about "great" white theologians. They were ordinary people, and most were not any smarter than me. I actually had an advantage because I knew their history and theology, but they didn't know mine. I could easily see the ideological "taint" in their theological claims, much more than they were willing to admit. And regardless of any discomfort I had caused among the faculty, I must have done alright. Shortly after my interview in January, I was offered an appointment as assistant professor of systematic theology at Union.

Black Theology and Black Power was published in March 1969. If it didn't make the *New York Times'* bestseller list, it was nevertheless an immediate event, widely reviewed in the news media, as well as in theological journals and church magazines. The book cover was blood red—symbolizing the blood shed by black people in America from slavery times to the era of civil rights and Black Power. Among black seminary students, professors, political activists, and preachers, everybody was talking about it. It was called "the Little Red Book."

Along with the invitation from Union, I also received offers from Colgate, San Francisco Theological Seminary, the University of California at Santa Barbara, and others. Seminaries and divinity schools around the country were feeling the heat, as black students demanded black professors and courses about black church studies. But, unlike Union, none of these schools was located in Harlem, the cultural center of the black world in the United States. As a black theologian, Harlem was a more appropriate and challenging place for me to teach and write. Besides, I wanted to teach where Niebuhr and Tillich had taught. If I could put black theology in the theological curriculum at Union, then it would be taken seriously throughout the world. Those were the main reasons I chose to teach at Union, even though I arrived without tenure and about half the salary that other places had offered. That is also the reason I have remained on the faculty nearly a half century later.

Union Seminary was a liberal school, well known for supporting outrageous, independent-thinking professors. It separated from the Presbyterian Church in the late nineteenth century in support of its professor, Charles A. Briggs (whose chair I would later hold), who was charged with heresy for not adhering to the inerrancy of scripture. It supported Niebuhr in his blast against Protestant liberalism and in his run for political office on the Socialist ticket. Dietrich Bonhoeffer had spent time there before returning to Germany. It also found a place for Tillich when he was fired from the University of Frankfurt during the Nazi era. But I knew that I would be pushing the boundaries in new ways.

During my interview at Union, the dean of students, Lawrence N. Jones, a Negro who received his Ph.D. from Yale Divinity School under the mentorship of H. Richard Niebuhr, Reinhold's brother, mentioned that I must feel honored just to find myself walking where Tillich and Niebuhr had walked—not to mention teaching where they taught. But I wasn't honored the way he thought I should be.

Niebuhr had expressed no moral outrage against lynching or segregation, even though he lived during that era. What happened to black people in the United States or in Africa was of little concern in his ethical value system. As for Tillich, shortly after my arrival at Union I asked a visiting speaker, Professor James Luther Adams, of Harvard Divinity School, who knew him well,[14] "Why didn't Tillich talk about racism in the United States the way he opposed Nazism in Germany?" Adams said Tillich was asked a similar question and replied that "his American audience would reject him." He meant his white audience, because he showed no interest in making his theology speak to the situation of black people.

How could I, a descendant of black slaves, be honored to teach at a school where white theologians ignored white supremacy? I respected the fact that Tillich and Niebuhr were brilliant theologians, but, to paraphrase Baldwin, there are a lot of brilliant theologians and most are irrelevant and some are evil.[15]

From the time C. Eric Lincoln read my first essay, "Christianity and Black Power" and my first book, *Black Theology and Black Power,* he had started telling the world about a young black theologian developing a black theology that would change how Americans think about the gospel and Black Power. Everybody was talking about the *need* for a black theology, but no one was writing it. At a symposium of the Institute of Religion at Howard University, J. Deotis Roberts said:

---

14. See James Luther Adams, *Paul Tillich's Philosophy of Culture, Science, and Religion* (New York: Harper & Row, 1965).

15. Margaret Mead and James Baldwin, *Rap on Race* (New York: Dell, 1971), 183.

There has not been in the history of this country a major contribution to theology by a Negro. . . . There has been no system of theology informed by a profound grasp of theology and Christian history by a Negro. The Negro in America has not produced . . . a Niebuhr. American-born theologians have been few, but three hundred years of American history have not witnessed one major Black Theologian.[16]

I was determined to fill that gap.

I was pleased to receive an invitation from the National Conference of Black Churches (NCBC) to join their organization and to participate in writing a statement on "black theology" at the Interdenominational Theological Center (ITC), a black seminary in Atlanta, Georgia (June 1969). I wrote the section on "What is black theology?" and defined it as "a theology of black liberation." Other invitations followed.

When a reporter from *Time* magazine asked me rhetorically, "Is not the idea of a black theology a fad?" I responded with passion. "Absolutely not! Black people are not a fad. We are not going anywhere, and nobody can speak for us. That includes white theologians. Black theology is nothing but black people speaking for themselves about God and the meaning of their struggle for dignity in the United States."

The oppressed claiming the right to do their own theology is always rejected by oppressors. I resolved to speak about God in a language that empowered black people to love their blackness and to reject whiteness. I was not going

---

16. J. Deotis Roberts, "The Black Caucus and the Failure of Christian Theology," *Journal of Religious Thought* (Summer Supplement 1969): 21.

to debate white theologians about whether I had the right to define theology. Who were they to tell me what theology is? They enslaved, lynched, segregated, and humiliated my people in every way they could. Now after all the evil they had done to black people, why should I listen to them talk about God and theology? To paraphrase Malcolm, when a young black told him he was studying to be a Catholic priest, "You've got to be out of your goddamn mind."[17]

Meanwhile, Eric Lincoln presented me with another challenge and opportunity. He told me he wanted me to replace him as a visiting professor of black history during the summer in the graduate program at the University of the Pacific in Stockton, California. I told him that I was trying to finish my second book for his series and preparing to move and teach at Union, and that I didn't know enough about black history to teach at a graduate level. As he had before, he simply said, "You can do it." That was it. After all the doors Lincoln had opened for me, I couldn't say "no."

So I went to Stockton. For eight hours a day, I read, wrote lectures, and taught black history, staying one step ahead of my students, while another eight were devoted to writing my book. I got very little sleep. But as it turned out, teaching black history helped me in my writing, and my writing assisted my teaching. Teaching black history to black and white master of arts students at the University of the Pacific made me feel like Br'er Rabbit "in the briar patch,"[18] my natu-

---

17. Lawrence Lucas, *Black Priest/White Church: Catholics and Racism* (New York: Random House, 1970), 12-13. "Are you out of your goddamn mind?" is what Malcolm actually said.

18. See "Tar Baby," in *The Book of Negro Folklore*, ed. Langston Hughes and Arna Bontemps (New York: Dodd, Mead, 1958), 1–2.

ral habitat. It also helped me to understand at a deeper level why history is so important for black liberation theology. Once again, a request from Lincoln had brought rewards beyond my anticipation.

At the same time, the black community in Stockton made me feel like I was back home in Bearden, Arkansas. They entertained my wife, Rose, and me in their homes, cooking collard greens and sweet potatoes, cornbread and chitterlings, making me feel like I was eating my mother's home cooking. We laughed and talked about blackness and white folk, which kept me grounded in what I was teaching and writing.

In July a story appeared in *Time* magazine about black theology. It included my photo, which came as a shock. I had no idea that black theology would reach a mainstream national audience. There was more attention coming to black theology, and to me, as its creator, than I'd ever imagined. I met with some of the Black Panthers in Oakland who had read *Black Theology and Black Power,* and I saw their creative Breakfast Program for children. We talked about religion and the black freedom struggle. I believed God was using them to shake up America, even though they did not speak of their work in that way.

When my course was over I left California, arriving in New York City on July 21. But terrible news awaited me. The desk attendant at McGiffert Hall at Union informed me that my father had died the previous night. Immediately, I departed for Bearden, Arkansas, to attend his funeral.

Given all the personal, political, and academic pressures I was facing that summer I don't know how I did it. But I finished writing *A Black Theology of Liberation* and submitted the manuscript to Eric Lincoln. I dedicated the book to my mother and to the memory of my father. He had been my role model. I was glad he had lived long enough to see the publication of my first book, and to know that he carried it around wherever he went. I felt the new book embodied both the political militancy my father lived as well as my mother's religious sensibility. She was closer to Martin Luther King Jr., a Christian, always looking for a way to conciliate, appealing to nonviolence and love. My father was more like Malcolm X, a militant, truth-speaking man, refusing to compromise the truth. The blood of both was running in my veins, and it was difficult for me to choose between them.

With my appointment at Union, the publication of my first book, and many public lectures around the country, black theology was beginning to be taken much more seriously, despite the controversy it generated in certain quarters. At a meeting of the Society of Christian Ethics, where I was invited to speak, the respondent, Professor Waldo Beach, of Duke University Divinity School, a well-known senior scholar, called black theology a "tribal theology," suggesting something primitive and savage. He did not even address the themes of liberation, black dignity, and white supremacy that shaped my theological perspective. I replied that "white theology is the real tribal theology because it talks only to itself, and is the most savage theological discourse I know, justifying slavery and colonization in the name of God and country."

I soon discovered that *most* white theologians couldn't talk about theology and race in a way that showed a real knowledge and respect for black people. They seemed interested only in seeing whether I knew enough about European theology to join their conversation.

Among the few exceptions were Beach's colleague at Duke Fred Herzog, and my Union colleague Paul Lehmann. Herzog risked alienation from many of his white colleagues for his support of black theology. As for Lehmann, no white theologian took black theology more seriously than he did.[19] Though he did not always agree with me, he listened and was transformed by our dialogue, reminding me of the debates I had had with my Garrett advisor, William E. Hordern.

Lehmann, Herzog, and Hordern were Barthians, and many of my critics said I was one, as well. Probably our mutual respect for Barth's theology contributed to our openness to one another. Like other Barthians, I was deeply Christological in my orientation. But unlike them, my focus on Jesus Christ was not derived from an intellectual engagement with the Bible or with the European Protestant Reformation or with twentieth-century neo-orthodox theology. Black theology's spirit did not come from Europe but from Africa, from American slavery and its auction blocks, from the spirituals and the blues. The Christocentric center of black theology was defined by the Black Christ who enabled black people to survive slavery, to overcome Jim Crow segregation, and to defeat the lynching tree. The Black Christ was a black slave and "a black body swinging in the southern breeze." Barth did not

---

19. See Paul Lehmann, *Transfiguration of Politics: The Presence and Power of Jesus of Nazareth in and over Human Affairs* (New York: Harper, 1974); and Paul Lehmann, "Black Theology and 'Christian' Theology," *Union Seminary Quarterly Review* 31, no. 1 (Fall 1975).

know about the Christ witnessed in the black experience. His "absolute qualitative distinction" between God's revelation and human initiative did not apply to the culture and history of oppressed people, because God became an exploited human being in Jesus of Nazareth, "taking the form of a slave," a black slave in the United States. Jesus the Christ "humbled himself and became obedient to the point of death—even death on a cross" (Phil 2:5–8), which in the United States was a lynching tree. God in Christ did not make an absolute distinction between divine revelation and the black experience but rather took that experience as God's own reality. That insight was as difficult for white people to grasp and understand as it was for Romans to see God revealed in a Jewish peasant or a crucified rebel. Lehmann wrestled with this claim, even though his idea of "Christian theology" was something separate from "black theology."

My first year at Union was exciting and memorable— teaching black liberation theology and lecturing about it all over the country, while getting to know new students and colleagues. Many senior members of the faculty did not take me seriously because they did not take black people seriously. Black theology was a marginal concern for them. The most important intellectual matters in theology and the Bible were defined in Europe, where most of them had studied. But I was not intimidated. Why should I bow to their arrogance? Jesus preached and taught about God's coming reign from the margins of the Roman Empire. I was proud to proclaim the gospel of black liberation from the margins of white culture. I strutted through the academic halls of Union as if I belonged there and nobody had better mess with me. White senior faculty didn't know what to make of me—wearing African dashikis and sporting a huge Afro, and looking mean and angry.

I will never forget the first student assembly during orientation week. A faculty panel of five was asked to respond to the question: "What is the central message of the Bible?" I spoke third. "The central message of the Bible is God's liberation of the poor from oppression," I said. "That theme is found in the exodus of ancient Israel from Egypt, in the prophets' message of justice, and most of all in Jesus's birth in a stable, his preaching of liberation and solidarity with the poor, and his death and resurrection. Liberation of the poor from the shackles of bondage is the central message of the Bible."

I stopped there. I wanted everybody to understand what I was saying—students and faculty. The moderator, a professor in patristics, turned to a senior biblical scholar, to respond. He could hardly speak because he knew I was right. "Liberation," he said, "is one theme but not the only one. There are many."

Before he could say another word, I interrupted him: "I accept the fact that there are many messages in the Bible. But no one can deny that liberation is its central theme. Is that not true?"

"Perhaps," he said.

It never ceased to amaze me how white scholars could quibble, making simple things more complicated than they really were. What is more central in the Christian Bible than the exodus and Jesus stories and the prophetic call for justice for the poor? Meanwhile, he kept appealing to technical biblical scholarship and recent archeological discoveries.

"Are you saying that ordinary Christians have to consult biblical scholars before they can know what the biblical message is?" I asked.

"No, no," he replied.

But students understood what I was saying, and they enrolled in my classes.

In the spring semester of my first year, I was invited back to Garrett to deliver the Harris Franklin Rall Lectures, a very distinguished honor, and one that I could not have imagined while I was a student. This invitation was mostly due to the pressure of Garrett's African American students and alumni. Trouble was brewing among blacks, and the white faculty and administrators had to make concessions. To return to the graduate school where I was the first Negro to receive a Ph.D., but the only student who did not receive a scholarship, was an experience that brought mixed emotions.

Nevertheless, standing before the Garrett Seminary audience, with professors, students, and alumni looking at me, was an amazing and rewarding experience. Philip S. Watson, my former advisor, introduced me. What he said was not memorable. I stood at the elevated lectern in the Chapel of Unnamed Faithful, paused, and looked at the people in the pews, wondering to myself how I had arrived at the point of delivering these prestigious lectures in the school where I had nearly been rejected from the doctoral program. Nevertheless, I collected myself and slowly began to speak from *A Black Theology of Liberation*, which was scheduled for publication that fall. The titles of my lectures were "Black Theology and the Afro-American Revolution" and "Black Theology and the Black Christ." I began my first lecture with the words:

Christianity is essentially a religion of liberation. The function of theology is that of analyzing the meaning of that liberation for the oppressed community so they can know that their struggle for political, social, and economic justice is consistent with the gospel of Jesus Christ. Any message that is not related to the liberation of the poor is not Christ's message. Any theology that is indifferent to the theme of liberation is not Christian theology. In a society where [people] are oppressed because they are *black*, Christian theology must become *Black Theology*, a theology that is unreservedly identified with the goals of the oppressed community and seeking to interpret the divine character of their struggle for liberation.[20]

Black students were thrilled with every word I said but whites were noticeably disturbed, especially my former professors. I could feel my advisor's anger, even though he didn't express it openly to me.

Afterward we went to lunch with two of his colleagues and my former teachers. It was bright and sunny, and we were talking about the beautiful day, the spring flowers and the chirping birds. I was in a good mood, with a warm and friendly smile, when Watson suddenly turned to me and said, "Jim, why don't you write and speak publicly with as generous an attitude as you are now displaying at lunch?"

My mood changed suddenly. I felt somewhat like James Baldwin, who wanted his stepfather's approval as a writer but never received it. I realized that I still wanted Dr. Watson's

---

20. Cone, *A Black Theology of Liberation*, 11.

approval of my black theological perspective, though he didn't get it, and probably never would.

"Dr. Watson," I replied, trying to speak with respect, as I would with my father, "it is impossible for me to display a generous attitude when I am thinking about lynched black bodies! If you were in my place, you wouldn't be generous either." Silence ensued. It was the last time we communicated until he retired, when I wrote an essay for his *Festschrift* and he wrote to thank me. I was glad to hear from him, but I could tell he wouldn't be able to understand what it was that made me so militant and uncompromising.

I returned to Union to complete an exciting first year of teaching, writing, and lecturing about black liberation theology. Everybody in the academy and the church seemed to have strong opinions about it—whether positive or negative.

CHAPTER 4

When He Put My Name on the Roll

Learning from My Critics

"There is no such thing as black theology," Charles H. Long shouted, pointing his finger at me, as if he were scolding a younger brother. The subject, at this gathering of the Society for the Study of Black Religion, was my new book, *Black Theology of Liberation*. Long rejected my basic premise. "Theology is a Western concept, created by Europeans to dominate and denigrate non-Western peoples," he said, "and thus completely alien to the black religious experience." Following Long's passionate outburst, the room went silent, as everyone waited to hear what I was going to say. Among this gathering of seasoned scholars, I was by far the youngest person present. I simply stared back, not knowing how to respond.

I respected Long and wanted him to be my teacher. I knew there was an important truth behind what he was saying, though I was damned if I understood exactly what it was. He seemed more interested in embarrassing me than teaching me, and no one else was coming to my defense. He continued: "If one is going to have a theology, it must arise from religion, something prior to theology."[1]

I'd expected white scholars to dismiss black theology, but hadn't expected that response from black scholars; I thought they'd come to my defense, but they didn't, and I felt alone and scared. I realized I had to think deeper about what I was doing. My critics inadvertently helped me to reflect on theology and the black experience in a more critical and complex way.

The Society for the Study of Black Religion (SSBR) became the academic context for the development and challenge of black theology. It was founded in 1970, one year after the publication of *Black Theology and Black Power*, through the initiative of Long, professor of the history of religions at the University of Chicago, and Charles Shelby Rooks, of the Fund for Theological Education, who became its first president. Both had invited me to be on the steering committee of six, because my book had played a major role in engaging black scholars in discussion about the meaning of black religion and theology. No whites were allowed to join because their issues distracted from what we wanted to discuss among ourselves.

In its early years, SSBR turned out to be a platform for Charles Long to launch his persistent and harsh criticism of black liberation theology. Whatever the subject, he would find a way to attack my books—an attack that continued throughout the 1970s and much of the '80s. No doubt much

---

1. See Charles H. Long, "Perspectives for a Study in Afro-American Religion in the United States" (1971), in Charles H. Long, *Significations: Signs, Symbols, and Images in the Interpretation of Religion* (Philadelphia: Fortress, 1986), 188.

of what he said was valid, and in fact I learned a great deal from him, even if I was often deeply offended. He was a powerful intellectual. His main point was: "Theologies are about power. . . . These discourses are about the hegemony of power—the distribution and the economy of this power in heaven and on earth. . . ."[2]

I did not then disagree with his essential point, nor do I now. But I was trying to create a new language about God that derived from the black experience and the struggle for justice and dignity, which I knew was not simply the flip side of white Western theology. While respecting Long's intellectual prowess, I also knew that there was truth in black theology, articulated by the civil rights movement, headed by Martin Luther King Jr., a black churchman and theologian, and Black Power, articulated by Malcolm X, a Muslim minister and the greatest defender of black dignity in the modern world.

Many years later, to my great surprise and still something of a mystery, Long offered a positive acknowledgment of my work in his important text *Significations* (1986): "James Cone's first book of 1969, *Black Theology and Black Power*, was the signal for a new mode of theological writing. . . . Its style is evocative and prophetic; its focus is the meaning of the oppressed as the focus of Christian theology. It appears within the historical context of the civil rights movement, and its avowed aim is to explicate the theological meaning of black power." Long never said anything like that in the SSBR meetings or to me. I really thought he hated everything I'd written. There was more:

---

2. Long, "Freedom, Otherness, and Religion: Theologies Opaque" (1986), in *Significations*, 209.

The programmatic intent of Cone's work has found expression in his *The Spirituals and the Blues, A Black Theology of Liberation,* several major articles, and his influence as a professor at Union Theological Seminary in New York where he has guided several students, as well as his influence and relationships with Third World and liberation theologians throughout the world. While rooted in the black American experience, his work and career seem destined to have catholic implications.[3]

In his later work, Long analyzed the significance of my work along with that of Vine Deloria Jr., an American Indian scholar, author of *Custer Died for Your Sins* (1969), *We Talk, You Listen* (1970), and *God Is Red* (1973).

The civil rights movement is the context in which Cone and Deloria present their work; it would be difficult to imagine these works apart from this context. It is at this point and upon this ground that they seize the initiative. They make it clear that though their works appear within the civil rights movement, their efforts should not be seen as a continuation of the American reformist apologetics of the perennial American dilemma. Neither have they attempted to conform to scholarly and popular stereotypes of their images on the American scene.[4]

Long continues: "Cone's *Black Theology and Black Power* is the first in a series of works that go on to explicate the meaning of blackness and power within structures of American

---

3. Ibid., 205.
4. Ibid., 206.

theology and culture. . . ."[5] He calls Deloria's and my works "opaque theologies," but questions whether there can be "theologies of the opaque," because of "an internal ambiguity." He correctly acknowledges that black liberation theology "is an accusation regarding the world view, thought structures, theory of knowledge . . . of the oppressors. The accusation is not simply of bad acts but, more important, of bad faith and bad knowledge. It is indeed a battle of theology. The polemics, rhetoric, and intellectual resources of the debate remind one of the Lutheran Reformation."[6]

Up to this point, I had no disagreement with Long: no one, in fact, has explicated the meaning of my writings with greater clarity. "But do the protagonists," he asks, "wish only to win a theological debate?" Absolutely not! Long recognized that winning a debate wasn't my intent. "They [Cone and Deloria] wish to claim or prepare a place and a time for the full expression of those who have suffered . . . oppression. Such a place and time would by implication free all human beings, even oppressors, for it is their consciousness and acts of oppression that constitute their unfreedom and inhumanity." Now we arrive at the crux of the issue for Long: "Is theological discourse appropriate for this intention?"[7] His answer was an unequivocal *no*.

As I see it, Long was still thinking of theology in a European mode, as language about power over the powerless. But Europeans can't tell powerless people what theology is or how to do it. Black theology is a language about God that comes out of black experience, and its meaning is found in

---

5. Ibid., 207.
6. Ibid., 208.
7. Ibid., 208–9.

its *style*. This marks the difference from white methodology, even though I'd used European theology to create a new black theological language, as slaves used white Christianity to create a new vision of their dignity. I wish that Long and I could have joined forces and engaged each other, like jazz musicians in a combo. But that was not to be. He was more interested in winning a debate, and he invariably succeeded. I couldn't engage in dialogue with him. I remained silent for several years before responding. When, finally, I did, I merely said, paraphrasing great Chinua Achebe: "If you don't like my books, write your own."[8]

While J. Deotis Roberts and Gayraud Wilmore agreed with Long, what they said was less vehement and harsh. I learned from them both, especially from Wilmore, who based his critique on his appreciation of my work and his involvement in the black church, the civil rights and Black Power movements. What J. Deotis Roberts criticized was my endorsement of Black Power, which he regarded as un-Christian, violent, lacking any interest in reconciliation with whites. It was not that I wasn't interested in such reconciliation, but I felt that first we must speak of black liberation, without which reconciliation had no real meaning. How could blacks be reconciled with people who act in ways that deny their humanity?

William Jones's *Is God a White Racist?* (1973) arose from the classical question of theodicy: If God is perfect in goodness and power, whence comes evil? If God is liberating black people from white supremacy, why are they still oppressed,

---

8. "If you don't like someone's story, write your own." Cited in Dwight Garner, "Bearing Witness, with Words," *New York Times,* March 23, 2013.

especially after nearly four hundred years of slavery, lynching, and Jim Crow segregation? When the problem of suffering is put that way, I can only say, "I don't know." Theology is not philosophy; it is not primarily rational language and thus cannot answer the question of theodicy, which philosophers have wrestled with for centuries. Theology is symbolic language, language about the imagination, which seeks to comprehend what is beyond comprehension. Theology is not antirational but it is nonrational, transcending the world of rational discourse and pointing to a realm of reality that can only be grasped by means of the imagination. That was why Reinhold Niebuhr said, "One should not talk about ultimate reality without imagination,"[9] and why the poet Wallace Stevens said, "God and the imagination are one."[10] Black liberation theology strives to open a world in which black people's dignity is recognized.

All these criticisms, though, missed the point that impelled me to write. I wasn't primarily trying to make an academic point about black religion, as Long and Wilmore suggested, nor about theodicy, as Jones advocated, or even about reconciliation, as Roberts recommended. What concerned me instead was to show that being black and Christian could be liberating. God calls us to be black because, as Baldwin said, "blackness is a tremendous spiritual condition, one of the greatest challenges anyone alive can face."[11] We don't have to

---

9. Cited in Richard Fox, *Reinhold Niebuhr: A Biography* (Ithaca, NY: Cornell University Press, 1996), 171.

10. Wallace Stevens, "Final Soliloquy of the Paramour," in *Selected Poems* (London: Faber and Faber, 1965), 143.

11. James Baldwin, "No Name in the Street" (1972), in *Collected Essays*, ed. Toni Morrison (New York: Library of America, 1998), 471.

apologize for blackness but should embrace it unapologetically and unashamedly.

Any critique that did not address black self-hate was beside the point. Malcolm was right: "The worst crime the white man has committed was to teach black people to hate themselves." Again, as Baldwin said, "All you are ever told in the country about being black is that it is a terrible, terrible thing to be. Now in order to survive this, you have to really dig down into yourself and re-create yourself, really, according to no image which yet exists in America." This is no easy task. But, as Baldwin continued, in an interview with Studs Terkel, "You have to . . . decide who you are, and force the world to deal with you, not their idea of you."[12] This is exactly what I was trying to do as a theologian. I felt that any criticisms directed at me were inconsequential as long as they did not address the most vexing problem in the black community—self-hate.

I wasn't writing for rational reasons based on library research; I was writing out of my experience, speaking for the dignity of black people in a white supremacist world. I was on a mission to transform self-loathing Negro Christians into black-loving revolutionary disciples of the Black Christ. I was singing a new theological song, a blues song, messing with theology the way B. B. King messed with music. I used Barth's theology the way B. B. used his guitar and Ray Charles used the piano. I had "my mojo working" (Muddy Waters) as I danced the way I felt in my flesh and bones. I wasn't following Barth; he was simply an instrument I played and left behind whenever it got in my way. I was following Ray Charles

---

12. James Baldwin, *Conversations with James Baldwin*, ed. Fred L. Standley and Louis H. Pratt (Jackson: University Press of Mississippi, 1989), 5–6.

because he made "me feel all right," "Black and Proud" (James Brown), and demanding "Respect" (Aretha Franklin).

Any critic who mattered would have to understand what set me on fire. White theology didn't set me on fire. Research in theology, biblical studies, history of religions, sociology, philosophy, or any other academic discipline interested me but didn't set me on fire. What was happening to black people in the urban centers of Chicago, Detroit, Los Angeles, and New York, and on the back roads of Alabama, Mississippi, Arkansas, and Georgia did that. It was the same things that set Martin and Malcolm on fire: black suffering. It was black fires burning in urban centers and at the foot of Southern lynching trees that created black theology.

Gayraud Wilmore was on fire for the same reason. That's why I could work with him, even though we often disagreed. Together we edited books about black theology and debated with each other and with others all over the world. Never once did I see any differences in our mission to address the need for black people to love themselves before they could begin to love others.

White critics soon ceased to matter to me at all. Black critics, at least, were in my world, and I could learn from them. But white critics lived in a privileged world that exploited black people and even the best of them missed what black people were struggling against daily—going to work, raising children, and forging meaning in a society that refused to recognize them as human beings. I am well known in some white theological circles for having said that white theologians should "shut their damn mouths." Some took that as an excuse to say nothing about white supremacy in theology, America, and the world. After more than nearly fifty years of working with, writing about, and talking to white theologians, I have to say that most are wasting their time and energy, so far as I am concerned. For me, the real issue, when talking with critics, black or white, is this: what will liberate black people to think for themselves, to fight for justice, and to embrace blackness? Justice and blackness are the heart of what black liberation theology is about.

People cannot live without a sense of their own worth. In black liberation theology, I was expressing black self-worth, which was denied or ignored by white theology and its churches. The black church, despite its failures, gives black people a sense of worth. They know they are somebody because God loves them and Jesus died for them. No matter what white people do to them, they cannot take their worth away. This is what the gospel means for black Christians, and that's why they go to church, no matter how corrupt their preachers might become. Black Christians worship God and not preachers. God bestows worth, gives them an infinite sense of meaning.

While I listened to my critics I refused to bow to them, even though they were right about many things. In debates with critics, I had to figure out what was true and what wasn't. Shaken by what certain black critics said, I went back to my slave grandparents, back to the auction blocks and slave ships, and all the way back to Africa. I could hear the sounds of music, drums beating, people dancing and singing, connecting with the spirits long dead. I soaked myself in "the world I came from"—the world of the spirituals and the blues, folklore, and slave narratives and found the language of freedom and liberation black slaves and ex-slaves sang and talked about. This historical research was new territory for me, and I knew Charles Long was right. "Those who have lived in the cultures of the oppressed know something about freedom that the oppressors will never know," he wrote. "But what expression would a freedom deriving from people who had indeed endured and overcome oppression make?" They would make music and tell stories about how they got over. "If this freedom is not to be simply the sentimental imitation of the lordship-bondage structure with a new set of actors, it would have to be a new form of freedom."[13] Exactly! Recognizing this, I decided to examine black freedom in the spirituals and the blues, the music I first heard in black churches and juke joints in Bearden, Arkansas.

I wrote *The Spirituals and the Blues* to show that black liberation theology was not, as Long had suggested, derived primarily from the European theology I studied in graduate school. Although European thinkers helped me to get started in theology, the idea of liberation and freedom did not come from them. Already free, they did not need to advocate historical liberation from oppression. In their theologies, freedom was an abstract and philosophical principle, lost in the realm of ideas. I had to bring them down to earth, to the ghetto, and compel their work to serve the black struggle for justice. Their theologies were not written for the African people Europe colonized; they wrote for the colonizers.

Writing *The Spirituals and the Blues,* while listening to Mahalia Jackson, B. B. King, and other artists, was a soulful and a soul-searching experience. Soulful because black music touched my deepest feelings and emotions. Soul-searching because it was self-penetrating—transforming my

---

13. Long, *Significations*, 210, 211.

language as I read about slaves who created music out of a pit of nothingness.

I remember as a child walking to Macedonia AME Church every Sunday on a gravel road with my mother and father and my two brothers. We were dressed in our Sunday best: Daddy, five-foot-nine inches tall and weighing one hundred forty-five, was wearing his only suit—brown double-breasted—white shirt, brown tie, and shoes to match; Mother, five-foot-seven, a little plump, was wearing a light blue dress, matching hat and shoes, the most beautiful woman in Bearden, I thought; boys were wearing neat dress pants and white opened-collar shirts, thinking more about the girls than spiritual matters.

Sunday was a special time in the week, the Lord's Day, when everybody wore their best and we heard preaching, praying, and singing that made heaven ring. "God is in this house," Reverend Hunter often began, "let us rejoice and be glad in it." Rejoice we did, with an ecstasy that witnessed to a freedom in church we didn't experience in the white man's society. We sang about that freedom in songs handed down from our ancestors.

> Oh Freedom! Oh Freedom!
> Oh Freedom, I love thee!
> And before I'll be a slave,
> I'll be buried in my grave,
> And go home to my Lord and be free.

Sometimes the people shouted, tapped their feet, waved their hands, responding to the Spirit who never failed to visit and soothe the people's hearts and strengthen their determination to "hold on to God's unchanging hands." I couldn't sing, but I could feel the Spirit moving in my flesh and bones. Without going back to Macedonia and reexperiencing what I felt as a child, I couldn't have written *The Spirituals and the Blues*. There was still a lot of joy; the Spirit was high, and I felt that I was in God's house "once more and again." Many people who'd been there when I was a child had gone to "glory"; but others were "yet alive," still praising the Lord for having kept them safe from "hurt, harm and danger," and that was no small achievement because "whitefolks were still on the loose."[14] And there were a few new faces. They all knew me as James Hal, Lucy and Charlie's boy, Cecil and Charles's little brother. Daddy had "crossed the river of Jordan" much too early, when he was only sixty-two, but Mother was still among the living, still strong in faith, "working on her soul's salvation."

I sat quietly in church, reminiscing of the time when I was a child, head in Mother's lap, listening to songs of sorrow and joy. Life is all mixed up like that and the Spirituals got both emotions, even in the same song.

> Nobody knows the trouble I've seen,
> Nobody knows my sorrow,
> Nobody knows the trouble I've seen,
> Glory Hallelujah!

As I heard it, the "trouble" is white folks, and the "Hallelujah" is a faith expression that white folks don't have the last word about life's ultimate meaning.

Before I could write about them, I had to know about the origin of the spirituals. I read white and black scholars, mostly historians, so I could know what their debates were

---

14. Toni Morrison, *Beloved: A Novel* (New York: Alfred A. Knopf, 1987), 180.

about. But debates were not my main interest. I had to know in my existential being what created them and why their meaning transcends time, place, and people. These songs are a gift to the world. Howard Thurman's *Deep River* (1945) and *The Negro Spiritual Speaks of Life and Death* (1947) spoke to what I experienced in Macedonia—books I read over and over, although I always wondered whether he would appreciate my interpretation of the spirituals.

One afternoon in 1972 or thereabouts, shortly after my book was published, Howard Thurman, then speaking in New York City at the National Conference of Black Churches (NCBC) annual convocation, sent for me. I was surprised and somewhat anxious about his invitation, wondering what he wanted with me. I knew I had a political and black edge in my writings that seemed to conflict with his main message of integration and universalism. I really didn't disagree with him, but I wasn't sure he knew that. I knew he had read *Black Theology and Black Power* because he used it as one of his "direct sources" in *The Search for Common Ground*.[15] His chapter "The Search in Identity" seemed partly to be a direct response to me (and Albert Cleage, author of *The Black Messiah* [1968]), emphasizing the "new mood," which accented "Black Power," "Black Christ," and "black is beautiful." Thurman didn't reject the new mood but was concerned "that to undertake to build community as a closed entity within the large society is not only suicidal but the sheerest stupidity."[16] I wondered whether he thought I was advocating a "closed entity" of blacks in America.

---

15. Howard Thurman, *The Search for Common Ground* (New York: Harper & Row, 1971). See "Acknowledgments," ix.
16. Ibid., 102.

I'd first heard Thurman speak on television at the Chicago Sunday Evening Club when I was a student at Garrett. He spoke slowly with long pauses between words and sentences, which mesmerized his audience. I was captivated by his intelligence and his speaking style. Benjamin Mays and Martin Luther King Jr. had spoken there—two other religious giants, like Thurman, who had inspired me. I thought about all three as I walked to Thurman's hotel room that afternoon. After answering my knock on the door, he invited me in, directing me to sit in a chair opposite from where he and his wife were sitting. Although I was a professor and the author of three widely read books, sitting in the presence of Thurman made me nervous. I never had a feeling like that when I met white scholars, no matter who they were.

But Thurman (like Mays, King, and Lincoln) *was* my ancestor, one of those who had paved the way for me. I didn't want to offend him in any way. Even though we might disagree, he deserved my respect, as a man who fought for racial justice, during a time it could have cost him his life. Thurman's books spoke to my head and heart—*Jesus and the Disinherited* (1949), *The Luminous Darkness* (1965), and the two volumes on the spirituals. He was my theological pioneer. His books had made mine possible, but did he know I realized that?

Dr. Thurman sat down next to Mrs. Thurman on the sofa, looked me in the eyes, and said, calmly and firmly: "You are doing important intellectual work, young man, and don't let anybody stop you! They will try with their harsh critiques or by ignoring you but don't let them. Both black and white people need you. That's all I wanted to tell you."

I was nearly speechless. Mrs. Thurman smiled and nodded with approval. I felt like a messenger from God was speaking to me. Thurman was a deeply spiritual man, and many people regarded him as their spiritual leader, a kind of guru. No one can imagine the impact his words had on me.

All I could say was, "Thank you, sir! What you think about my books means everything to me. I would not be able to write without your writings and ministry. I can't tell you how pleased I am that you regard what I am doing as worthwhile."

I wish I could have engaged him in a theological conversation about his books and what he found in mine. What did he see as the strengths and weaknesses in my writings? It was one thing for Thurman to encourage me and quite another to have a critical conversation with him. I could have learned a lot from one of the great spiritual masters in the black religious experience. But at that time, I didn't have enough self-confidence to talk with him about what I wanted to ask.

These encounters with Mays, Lincoln, and Thurman transformed my life as a scholar. Each happened at the right time and place. The encounter with Mays showed me what my life could be before I'd even imagined it. The encounter with Lincoln was an affirmation that my first essay was worthwhile, encouraging me to stay the course, work hard, and be myself. The encounter with Thurman was also an affirmation of the books I'd written, letting me know that my ancestors were pleased.

Nothing pleased me more about *The Spirituals and the Blues* than the review written by Benjamin Mays.[17] He said that my book "gives a constructive and useful interpretation of Black music. His approach is creative." He concludes: "Professor

---

17. Benjamin Mays, review of *The Spiritual and the Blues, Union Seminary Quarterly Review* 28, no. 31 (Spring 1973): 257–58.

Cone's book deserves to be widely read by both blacks and whites. His interpretation of the blues and the spirituals gives the reader insights into the social, economic, and political life of Black people. It gives the sophisticated religious person an appreciation for the blues which are but another dimension of the spirituals, both helping the Black man to survive in a hostile world."[18] Reading Mays's review made me feel that I had become the scholar he'd told me I could be. I wondered whether he remembered inviting me to breakfast eight years before his review and what he'd told me then. Because of the harsh criticism I received from black scholars in the SSBR, I had assumed that anyone associated with the civil rights movement, defined by Martin Luther King Jr., would be critical of my respect for Malcolm X and Black Power.

I encountered Thurman only once and Mays twice. The last time I saw Dr. Mays was at the annual meeting of the SSBR in Atlanta in the early 1980s. He was the main speaker but became unexpectedly ill. While making his presentation he nearly fell to the floor and had to be taken immediately to a hospital. I was asked to read his prepared text, which I did. No one at the meeting knew of my connection with Mays and thus why it was such an honor to read his lecture. He survived his illness but died a few years later.

Of the three black figures in my early intellectual life, however, C. Eric Lincoln was by far the most important. He not only published my first essay in his edited book *Is Anybody Listening to Black America?* but also introduced me to the Union faculty and got my first two books published. But even more important, he was someone I could talk with

---

18. Ibid., 258.

about anything, seeking his personal counsel, whether that concerned my personal or professional life, writing issues, or the faculty culture at Union.

We were traveling in his car in upstate New York when I told Lincoln that I wanted to be a scholar and writer like him. He smiled, thanked me for the compliment, and then said emphatically, "No, you shouldn't want to be like me but *be yourself!* Be the best you can be. You have a distinct and creative voice." That was the best professional counsel anyone ever gave me. I meditated on Lincoln's advice and accepted it fully. It liberated me from trying to emulate anyone and worrying whether I was as talented a writer and scholar as my peers. I concentrated on developing the intellectual talents I was born with. I vowed to myself that no one would ever be able to say that I didn't realize my potential. Even today, I still feel that I can become a better writer, better scholar, and better teacher. I will work at getting better until I die. I owe Lincoln much more than I was able to tell him.

As for my critics, Long, Wilmore, Roberts, and Jones also transformed my intellectual life with their challenges, questions, and critiques. Nothing helps a writer or scholar to improve his or her craft more than worthy critics, and I was blessed in this regard. They motivated me to write not only *The Spirituals and the Blues* (1872) but also *God of the Oppressed* (1975), my fourth theological treatise in six years.

In *God of the Oppressed*, I was singing both the spirituals and the blues, preaching sermons in church, and signifying on the corner at the juke joint. It was an intellectual culmination of what I began in my blue room in Adrian and my brother's church in Little Rock. I put everything in this book, and left it all on the page. I told stories about Br'er Rabbit and Br'er Bear, Br'er Fox and Ole Sis Goose and about Stack-alee and High John the Conqueror, coming from Africa, "walking on the waves of sound." I answered critics and sometimes was not kind in the language I chose. As I read it now, I was a little too self-confident, bordering on theological arrogance. I was still young and hadn't acquired the humility that comes with age. But my arrogance was nothing like the arrogance of white theologians and blacks who sympathized with them. I was determined to write and say publicly what I thought about white people and do it not primarily for myself but for poor black people who couldn't speak for themselves and whose wisdom whites ignored.

Black theology shouldn't, indeed couldn't, rely strictly on religious sources in the narrow church sense, because secular sources were also a part of the black community. That was why I was pleased, though somewhat uneasy, when the Black Panthers had shown an interest in *Black Theology and Black Power*. There were tensions between us because I was a preacher and they didn't like preachers. They said that ministers got in the way and impeded the black revolution for which they believed they were the vanguard. They liked what I said about the revolutionary Black Christ. However, we never became soul mates.

I developed a much better relationship with black nationalists. During my first year at Union, Amiri Baraka (LeRoi Jones) called and invited me to visit him in Newark. His writings influenced me more than any nationalist, except for Malcolm X. I had read many of his poems, plays, and essays. I accepted his invitation and made my way to Newark where he was engaged in a heated campaign to elect Kenneth Gibson as the city's first black mayor. Baraka had read

Black Theology and Black Power, which opened our dialogue. A man small in stature but gifted with language, he loved my focus on blackness, though I could tell that my Christian identity didn't sit well with him. He organized the Congress of African Peoples, and at its first major conference, he asked me to be the co-chair of the religion workshop, along with Albert Cleage. There were nearly three hundred people in the workshop, and I was the only openly declared Christian, since Cleage could not attend. Leading a workshop of religious black nationalists, with many different views, was one of my challenging experiences.

Black nationalists urged me to denounce Christianity as the white man's religion because it was against the black revolution. I stood my ground and responded that Jesus was not white but a dark-skinned Hebrew who died fighting for the freedom for his people. We could learn a lot from Jesus. "Since you are critical of everything the white man says," I challenged them, "why are you so accepting of his interpretation of Jesus the Christ. Jesus was not who the white man says; he was crucified as an insurrectionist against the Roman state. Jesus had a lot in common with the black revolution today."

Although black nationalists were not convinced by my argument, they listened and hit back at me harder, testing my willingness to pick up a gun in defense of the black revolution. I firmly said no! "You can count me out on that. If you reject Christians because they will not engage in violence, then I say to you that I'm not for any revolution that does not include my mother, and she is a nonviolent Christian." We concluded the religion workshop with each group holding fast to its self-assured faith.

My dialogues with Black Panthers and black nationalists

strengthened my faith as a Christian. They were my "self-interrogation," to use the language of Rowan Williams: "When it is God that we are talking about, the need for such self-interrogation becomes more urgent, since dangers of avoiding it are so dramatic."[19] Both Panthers and nationalists gave me a much-needed self-interrogation.

The blues are a kind of self-interrogation for Christians who sing spirituals. They are "secular spirituals." As a child, I couldn't go to the juke joint, but I listened to gutbucket blues from a safe distance and on radio and danced to them at social events at school. The blues moved me as deeply as the spirituals. Little Milton was my favorite.

> If I don't love you baby,
> Grits ain't grocery,
> Eggs ain't poultry,
> And Mona Lisa was a man.

The spirituals transported blacks to a transcendent realm often called heaven, but the blues kept their feet on earth where love and sex defined the relation between a man and a woman. In both cases they had to deal with white supremacy.

> I'd rather drink muddy water, sleep in a hollow log,
> Dan to stay in this town, treated like a dirty dog.
> Sitting here wondering would a matchbox hold my
>   clothes,
> I ain't got so many, and I got so far to go.
> I've got a mind to ramble, a mind to leave this town.

---

19. Rowan Williams, *Dostoevsky: Language, Faith, and Fiction* (Waco, TX: Baylor University Press, 2011), 45.

The "low down dirty blues" gave black people a dignity they couldn't find at church. Blues people couldn't stand the church's "pie-in-the-sky" religion. They got drunk to ease their existential pain and had sex "in the midnight hour" (Wilson Pickett) to experience erotic ecstasies. Both God's music (spirituals) and the devil's music (blues) excited blacks and made them move spontaneously and uncontrollably. They often competed with each other, but deep down in the depths of black being, we knew that both came from the same bedrock experience, the experience that also gave birth to Black Panthers, black nationalists, and black theology. They were responses to the hardness of life, the absurdity of being black in a crazy white world. Blacks searched for meaning where there was none, but they refused, through the doggedness of their spirit, to accept that their lives meant nothing. They sang the blues and the spirituals, Saturday night and Sunday morning. Singing about life's absurdity was their testimony that they hadn't been defeated by the "trials and tribulations" in this world. They were " 'buked and scorned" and "talked about show's you're born." They knew "trouble all over this world." But they also knew that they were human beings, which gave them meaning no one could take away. "You treat me like a mule and I came out like a man."[20]

I published four books on black liberation theology between 1969 and 1975 and many essays during the same period, making my case, defending black theology against black and white critics, and challenging black churches to address self-hate in their preaching and their worship. They

20. Cited in James H. Cone, *God of the Oppressed* (Maryknoll, NY: Orbis Books, 2008), 12, from H. A. Baker Jr., *Long Black Song* (Charlottesville: University of Virginia Press, 1972), 116.

were all published more than forty years ago in the social and the political context of the civil rights and Black Power movements. I stood alone. As I look back, I know that I did not make it easy for either my allies or my critics. I was not going to be side-tracked with sophisticated, intellectual issues by black and white scholars. Howard Thurman, Benjamin Mays, and Eric Lincoln reinforced in me that I was doing the right thing. I was determined to write about black dignity in a language that ordinary African Americans would know that I was speaking their truth. I don't deny that Charles Long's analysis of black religion was important, but it was so sophisticated and nuanced that it took me some time before I knew exactly what he was talking about. Using words and phrases like "opaque," "opacity of reality," "oppugnancy," and "the methodological and philosophical meaning of transparency as a metaphor for a theory of knowledge" would confuse most blacks, as it did me, and would not speak to their spiritual condition. For me, everything I wrote addressed respect, and that still is my main concern.

Saul Bellow said: "What a man overcomes is a measure of his character." I overcame Jim Crow segregation in Arkansas to become widely known as the Father of Black Liberation Theology and a full professor at Union at thirty-four. But that was nothing compared to what my ancestors endured and overcame—246 years of chattel slavery, another 100 of segregation and lynching and white supremacy in every aspect of American life. In the midst of continued mental and physical brutalization, they created music that traveled the world—not just the spirituals and the blues but jazz and gospel, soul music and hip hop. I got my spiritual and intellectual strength from my ancestors. I am proud to be a part of their heritage.

CHAPTER 5

When He Saved My Soul

Learning from My Students

"Dr. Cone, you don't know a God damn thing about the gay experience!" a white male student shouted at me from the back of the room in my "Foundations in Christian Theology" class. I stopped speaking and looked straight at him. What flashed into my mind was the similar outburst I had made twenty years earlier in a class taught by my advisor, Dr. Watson. But unlike my advisor, I wasn't angry; I knew he was right, and that he was hurting from homophobia in the midst of the AIDS crisis in the 1980s, as I was from racism in the 1960s. Although I was trying to address homophobia in society, churches, and theology, he needed more. Silence filled the room, and I had to break it.

"You are right!" I replied, my eyes still focused on him. "I don't know much about the gay experience, but I know enough to talk about theologies emerging out of struggles of gays and lesbians for justice, initiated by the Stonewall Rebellion (June 1969). They found their voices at Union—especially Carter Heyward, Beverly Harrison, and Gary Comstock. I'm just getting started in my study of those who speak from the underside of history and, which, like the voices of black theology, are not even heard in dominant Western theology. Oppressed people have a right to speak about ultimate reality out of their own experience. That's why I began writing about God and the black experience. But since blacks are not the only oppressed people, it is my responsibility to include many voices of the oppressed people who have to fight for dignity, even though I don't know as much about them as I know about black people. Jesus's story empowered me to write about what he means for blacks struggling for dignity; now I want you to do the same. I cannot speak for you but I hope I can inspire you to find your voice, as I found mine. That's why I teach."

I paused, as the rest of the class listened attentively, while I kept my eyes focused on the young man before me. "Your anger is how theology begins. It starts with anger about a great contradiction that can't be ignored. That's what happened to Athanasius in the fourth century, Luther in the sixteenth, and Barth in the twentieth. It also happened to me. If I had not been angry about white supremacy, I would not have written anything. You are angry, and I understand that. I'm still angry. But anger alone is not enough. You must use it to speak out and to write as creatively as you can, about the fire burning in you. Go to the root of your experience and articulate what no one can express except people who hurt like you. That's what I did. You can do it too."

Union is well known for the diversity of its student body. It makes for a challenging teaching experience, but I love it. There were gays, lesbians, and queers, blacks and whites, straight women and men, and people of color from many U.S. communities and other countries looking at me. I wanted to speak to everyone, not just to a white gay student; what I was saying to him was meant for all.

"One writes out of one thing only—one's own experience," wrote James Baldwin, a gay black artist who came out of the closet in the 1940s when it wasn't safe to do so, twenty years before Stonewall. I repeated Baldwin's quote several times for emphasis. "When I embraced the black experience," I told the class, "I began to write. That's what you must do: Embrace your experience! Then write your heart out. But you must talk to others about their experience, and become voracious readers of your stories and theirs and stories and sayings of people around the world." I could feel all my students looking at me.

I returned to the student whose interruption had created this teaching moment. "I'm not including what gay and lesbian people say in this course because I want to patronize them. I am including them because their struggle for dignity is my struggle too. My teaching is defined by my love of all my students and that includes white students, especially marginalized white students. I know what it means to be marginalized, ignored, and despised. I was born in a society that despised me for being who I am—black! I know something of what you are feeling because there is a connection between blackness and gayness."

I continued, "'Jesus is black,' I have often said. But we could also say Jesus is gay and any other identity being humiliated. One of my students, Jacquelyn Grant, said, 'Jesus is a black woman,' and she is right. Jesus is a way of talking about God's solidarity with people who are hurt and despised. For the same reason, we have to talk about the Stonewall uprising and those who spoke about it. Theology is always a second step, as Gustavo Gutiérrez and other Latin American liberation theologians have shown. Theology emerges in response to the struggle for justice among communities of the poor."

The class hour was nearing its end. "Suffering can separate us," I said, "or it can bring us together. It can become a bridge that connects people with one another, as Baldwin repeatedly said throughout his life. Martin Luther King Jr.'s life is also a witness to the interconnectedness of people. He said: 'All life is interrelated. All [people] are caught up in an inescapable network of mutuality, tied to a single garment of destiny. Whatever affects one directly affects all indirectly. I can never be what I ought to be until you are what you ought to be and you can never be who you ought to be until I am who I ought to be. This is the interrelated structure of reality. Injustice anywhere is a threat to justice everywhere.'"

Before the class ended, I reached out once more to the student who interrupted me. "If you want to help me understand the gay experience at a much deeper level than reflected in my teaching," I said to him, "give me a recommended reading list and talk to me about what you and others want to happen in this class. I am always ready to listen to students who are searching for meaning in their lives."

After class, the white gay student waited patiently as several students talked to me. After everyone had left he came up to me and thanked me for encouraging him to find his voice. He went on to write out a list of books, and later spent hours talking to me over the course of the semester. To this day, we remain good friends. He earned his doctorate, writing his dissertation on the gay experience and eco-justice, and is now a prominent voice in the LGBTQ community.

Student interruptions happen often at Union. Even when they're upsetting, we can use them as an occasion for teaching something that matters far more than the readings on our syllabus. I challenge students to speak for themselves as they struggle for dignity. When I was a student no one ever urged me to reflect on God using the black experience. It took me years after that to find my voice, since I didn't think that blacks had said or done anything worthy of theological reflection. When I discovered how wrong I was, I decided to share my excitement with other marginalized people.

Whether theologians acknowledge it or not, all theologies begin with experience. Theologians from the Western theological tradition often regard their theology as universal, something that everyone must study. But no theology is universal—neither Augustine's *City of God*, nor Aquinas's *Summa Theologiae*, Calvin's *Institutes,* nor Barth's *Church Dogmatics.* We are all particular human beings, finite creatures, and we create our understanding of God out of our experience. Hopefully, our own experience points to the universal, but it is never identical with it. For when we mistake our own talk about God with ultimate reality, we turn it into ideology.

While teaching theology, I urge students to be suspicious of absolutism in anything they say about God. One's own voice is far more important than simply repeating theologies in the Western tradition. No theologian—past or present—can replace the need to do theology for one's self, as Niebuhr did, and Augustine before him. We must do the same for our time and place, while recognizing the limitations not only of what others say but also what we ourselves say.

Teaching is profoundly connected with love. Without love for one's students, it is impossible to teach effectively. Such love is not "emotional bosh," as Martin King often said, in reply to people who questioned whether it was practical to "love one's enemy." Following King, Baldwin reminded Americans that "love is a battle, love is war; love is growing up. . . ."[1] As a teacher, I have had to be willing to struggle with my students and they with me and through our battle with each other we both could grow up—teaching each other to become the best human beings we could be. Love is always a "two-way street." We have to make each other see what we wouldn't see without each other. "Love is a battle" because we often don't want to see what someone is trying to make us see.[2] Jesus was trying to make people see the coming of God's justice. Those who refused to see it crucified him. Malcolm was trying to make Negroes and whites see the beauty and humanity of blackness; and those who refused to see that killed him. King was trying to make the world see that peace can be achieved only through nonviolence, and violent people assassinated him. Prophets are often killed for speaking a truth people don't want to hear.

"Systematic Theology 103: Foundations in Christian Theology" became my signature course at Union. I put my mind and heart, body and soul into it because it was a course taken by most students during their first semester. I wanted to show them that theology matters—that it's not merely an academic requirement but an intellectual and spiritual search for ultimate meaning in their lives. We read about Augustine's search

---

1. James Baldwin, "Nobody Knows My Name," in *Collected Essays*, ed. Toni Morrison (New York: Library of America, 1998), 220.

2. See especially James Baldwin, *Conversations with James Baldwin*, ed. Fred L. Standley and Louis H. Pratt (Jackson: University Press of Mississippi, 1989), 156.

in his *Confessions,* and Malcolm's in his *Autobiography.* We are all searching for meaning. That is why people come to Union and why I teach here. Some, like Augustine, will find meaning in the Christian faith, the focus of my course. But others, like Malcolm, will find it in Islam, and still others in other faith traditions. As Mircea Eliade wrote, "Life is not possible without an opening toward the transcendent; human beings cannot live in chaos. Once contact with the transcendent is lost, existence in the world ceases to be possible. . . ."[3]

I begin the course with questions: What is theology, and why does it matter? Theology is thinking about God who escapes our comprehension. What does it mean to reflect on an ultimate reality that can't be grasped? Why does it matter to think about that? Students need to know that theology is paradoxical language with no easy answers to ultimate questions, and that we need imagination to think about transcendent reality. What we call "God-talk" is imaginative language, like poetry, not rational language, even though Western theologians, following Greek philosophy, defined theology as rational thinking about God or what the eleventh-century philosopher-theologian Anselm called "faith seeking understanding." But seeking to understand the God of Jesus by means of Greek ideas has always been difficult. Jesus was a Jew from Nazareth, born to an impoverished unwed woman, who preached in the tradition of the Hebrew prophets, declaring divine solidarity with the poor and weak. His language was not philosophical or rational like that of Plato and Plotinus, but prophetic and apocalyptic, like the language of Isaiah and John the Baptist.

---

3. Mircea Eliade, *The Sacred and the Profane* (New York: Harper Torchbook, 1961), 34.

In the course we go on to examine ways Christians have interpreted the meaning of Jesus for their lives, following an intellectual inquiry focused primarily on voices from the underside of history, like that of Vine Deloria, a Native American writer, lawyer, and activist, along with other voices from Latin America, Asia, and Africa, and other marginalized groups in the United States, including feminist, womanist, and LGBTQ communities. Traditionally, theology has been "written with white hands," wrote Leonardo Boff, a leading Latin American liberation theologian. But in the second half of the twentieth century, many marginalized voices broke their silence and revolutionized the teaching of theology as Christians engaged the Bible though the eyes of those who are poor and oppressed.

The most influential Third World voices came from Latin America, with Gustavo Gutiérrez of Peru leading the way in his now-classic text, *A Theology of Liberation* (1973). He not only influenced other Latin American theologians, but also many in Asia, Africa, Europe, and the United States. At the same time, Gutiérrez was influenced by many others, especially feminists regarding gender, indigenous people on popular religion, and blacks on race. Gutiérrez and I learned a lot from each other in 1976 when we taught a course together at Union called "Theology from the Underside of History." Subsequently, we deepened our exchange with each other and with other religious thinkers in the Ecumenical Association of Third World Theologians (EATWOT). We visited each other's continents, talked about our similarities and differences, and expanded our knowledge of racism, classism, sexism, and cultural exploitation. From 1976 to 1996, I traveled the world, speaking in Africa, Asia, and Latin

America about black liberation theology and learning from others about poverty, indigenous religions, and the global reach of white supremacy in the world. It is one thing to read books about poor people but another to meet them where they live and struggle, sharing stories, talking about justice and life's ultimate meaning with confidence, in the hope that they can make their own future.

Teaching theology at Union brought its particular challenges. I became widely known as the Father of Black Theology, a topic no one had imagined would have an enduring presence in a seminary curriculum. Initially, white faculty thought it was just a fad, an "ephemeral explosion," as John Bennett put it, shortly after my arrival. "I do not doubt that it [black theology] will soon be dated,"[4] he wrote. That was easy for him to say since, for him, nothing was at stake. But black theology was in my DNA, and I was determined to show that Bennett and other white faculty were wrong when they dismissed its significance. It was like dismissing what black people think and believe about themselves and their gods. "I *know* my gods are real," wrote James Baldwin, "they have enabled me to withstand you."[5] Black theology is not something I invented; rather it derives from nearly four hundred years of black struggle for dignity and justice.

I knew that mentoring black students would be crucial for the survival of black theology, but I also knew I couldn't

---

4. John Bennett, "Black Theology of Liberation," in *Black Theology: A Documentary History, Volume 1: 1966–1979*, ed. Gayraud S. Wilmore and James H. Cone (Maryknoll, NY: Orbis Books, 1979), 178. Excerpt from Bennett's book *The Radical Imperative* (Philadelphia: Westminster, 1975), 119–31.

5. Baldwin, "No Name in the Street," in *Collected Essays*, 383. Emphasis in Baldwin.

do it alone. Since its founding in 1836, Union Seminary had not accepted a single black person into its doctoral program before I arrived in 1969. Apparently, no white faculty seemed concerned about this. They accepted the racist idea that while blacks could preach and sing, they couldn't, unlike whites, think and write with intellectual sophistication. When I asked my white colleagues why they had never accepted any blacks in the doctoral program in theology, they said, as I anticipated, that they couldn't find anyone qualified. "Are you saying that blacks are intellectually inferior or that you have not designed a doctoral program that meets their needs?"

"What can we do, Jim?" they asked.

I told them: "We have got to let black people know that theology is for them, good for their struggle for justice, and that Union is willing to change to meet their needs." After that, Union Seminary made significant changes in its understanding of the subject of theology and thereby became internationally known as the birthplace of black liberation theology and womanist theology, as well as feminist and other liberation theologies. More than forty students (men and women) received their doctorates under my direction. I am proud of the theological field at Union for being open to more than the study of European theology. Other fields slowly opened their areas of study to black and other minority students but did very little to attract significant numbers, because they didn't change the subject and the way it was taught. It was as if they said to blacks, "You can learn what we teach if you are smart enough, but we will not allow you to ask new questions as defined by the black experience."

No theology can survive without advocates who teach and write about it and without a church community that celebrates and preaches it. The National Council of Black Churches

(NCBC), now defunct, played an important role in introducing the black church community to the importance of embracing blackness and replacing the "white Christ" with the "black Christ," and writing important statements on "Black Power" (1966) and "Black Theology" (1969). NCBC's membership was comprised mostly of militant young ministers and scholars deeply involved in churches. While NCBC did not create black liberation theology, it was the spiritual force that sustained it during the early years of its development.

Besides recruiting black students to the doctoral program, Union also recruited other black faculty. Among those who joined me were James Washington (African American church history), James Forbes (preaching), Cornel West (philosophy of religion) and Samuel K. Roberts (sociology of religion). Together we changed the intellectual culture, making the study of black history and culture, black religion and theology central to Union's identity. West became an internationally known public intellectual and Forbes achieved great distinction as a powerful preacher, serving for many years as the pastor of Riverside Church across the street from Union. Unfortunately, Washington's death at an early age occurred just as he was making his mark as a leading scholar in African American religious history. Samuel K. Roberts left shortly after he arrived to become a highly regarded professor of sociology of religion at Union Theological Seminary (now Union Presbyterian Seminary) in Richmond, Virginia.

Cornel West was an intellectually exciting and an electrifying teacher. Students flocked around him in hallways and filled his classes. Faculty members were amazed by the exceptional range of his intellect. Jointly we taught a class on

"Black Theology and Marxist Thought."[6] I learned a lot from him about Marxism. We debated the relative importance of race and class in determining black people's powerlessness in the United States. While acknowledging that "race matters" (the title of his later bestselling book),[7] West contended that class mattered more. "Class position contributes more than racial status to the basic form of powerlessness in America," he wrote in *Prophesy Deliverance!*[8] He could be right, as religious thinkers from Latin American have also claimed, but I couldn't agree. People's actions are based less on science or reason than on emotions. Niebuhr is right: "Mind is the servant of impulse."[9] That's why poor white people often vote against their economic and political interest, preferring to vote with the white ruling class rather than joining with poor blacks to challenge them. Unless we deal with how people make decisions, whatever else is involved—whether race, class, gender, or something else—doesn't really matter.

Black women's criticism was much sharper than any coming from whites or black men, and none was sharper and truer than the criticism of Delores Williams, who took her first theology course with me during the early 1970s. She was a brilliant student, and we worked together until her interest focused with an equal emphasis on literature, which wasn't my area of competence. Even then, her theological voice had

---

6. See also his essay, Cornel West, "Black Theology and Marxist Thought," in *Black Theology: A Documentary History, Volume 1: 1966–1979*, 409.

7. See Cornel West, *Race Matters* (Boston: Beacon Press, 1993).

8. Cornel West, *Prophesy Deliverance! An Afro-American Revolutionary Christianity* (Philadelphia: Westminster, 1982), 115.

9. Reinhold Niebuhr, *Reflections on the End of an Era* (New York: Charles Scribner's Sons, 1934), 17.

an edge to it, and her intellectual power was developing into a force with which black theology would have to reckon. I knew it wouldn't be pleasant. Soon Jacquelyn Grant and Kelly Brown Douglas joined Williams on the graduate program in theology. Together they laid the intellectual foundation for womanist theology, with Katie Cannon adding her voice in social ethics.

No matter how hard I tried to listen to these "outrageous, audacious, and courageous or *willful*" black women, "committed to the survival and wholeness of entire people, male and female,"[10] I didn't have the experience or knowledge to really hear what I needed to hear. Williams, who later joined the Union faculty, argued that neither the paradigms of white feminist theology nor the liberation theme of black (male) theology adequately spoke to the experience of African American women. To illustrate her point, she turned to the biblical story of Hagar, Abraham and Sarah's bondswoman, forced to serve as a surrogate mother to Ishmael before being driven into the wilderness. In African American women's history and culture, Hagar is a powerful image, and Williams resurrected it in religious discourse. God didn't liberate Hagar, Williams reminded me, but was present with her in the wilderness, enabling her to procure survival and quality of life with her son, Ishmael. "What do you have to say about that, Mr. Black Theologian?" I could hear her caustic retort.

Later she developed her thinking in a ground-breaking

---

10. For a full definition of womanist, see Alice Walker, *In Search of our Mothers' Gardens: Womanist Prose* (New York: Harcourt Brace Jovanovich, 1983), xi. See also Walker's *The Color Purple* (New York: Pocket Books, 1982), which was made into a powerful movie by Stephen Spielberg.

text, *Sisters in the Wilderness: Womanist God-Talk* (1993), which elaborated on the intersectional dimensions of race, sex, and class that form the reality of African American women. She knew the biblical evidence, and black women's experience had much to add that we had not noted. "Furthermore," she said, "Moses' and Israel's liberation out of Egypt led to the genocide of the Canaanites, which is what happened to Native Americans in the United States." Liberation is a deeply problematic theme, with many ethical and religious contradictions. Although it's a prominent biblical theme, I now saw clearly its ambiguities.

These were difficult questions and issues. I had no answers. I still don't. The Bible is full of ethical and religious contradictions. What kind of God is it who would command Abraham to sacrifice his son, Isaac? I remember wincing when I heard and read about it as a child. Would my father obey such a command? I trembled to think he might, but I knew he wouldn't. That is why we cannot accept biblical inerrancy or literalism: there's no creative future on that road. Instead of worshiping the Bible, we regard it instead as an inspiring human book with which we wrestle, knowing that we may be wounded, as was Jacob when he wrestled with the angel. I am "perplexed" by all the ethical contradictions Williams identified "but not driven to despair" (2 Cor 4:8). Perplexity keeps me from being too sure of any religious claim I make. Faith needs doubt.

Williams's most potent and important critique centered on Jesus's death on the cross, which Christians identify as God's work of salvation. Jesus, they say every Sunday, died on the cross for them—preaching and testifying that he "[gave] his life as a 'ransom for many'" (Mark 10:45). The cross is the most powerful symbol in the Christian tradition. I grew up singing, "Jesus Keep Me Near the Cross," "the Old Rugged Cross," "Am I a Soldier of the Cross," "Must Jesus Bear the Cross Alone," and the great communion hymn, "There Is a Fountain Filled with Blood, Drawn from Emmanuel's Veins." But Williams would have nothing to do with blood talk, glorifying God killing Jesus, the Son of God, which the German theologian, Jürgen Moltmann, seemed to embrace in *The Crucified God* (1973). There is no salvation in the cross, Williams claimed, no "power in the blood." God didn't save anybody through Jesus's death. Salvation comes through Jesus's "ministerial vision" and his resurrection, and not through a bloody cross. Theologians, preachers, and Christians in general should stop worshiping Jesus's crucifixion. It's evil, pure and simple, she argued.

I knew Williams was right to reject the atonement theories of Anselm and Abelard and others in the Western theological tradition. But was she right to reject Jesus's cross, insisting that it has no significance for salvation? I felt much more needed to be said, but I wasn't sure what to say. Theology is paradoxical, symbolic, and poetic language, full of mystery. Its truth is found in imagination, and it speaks more to the heart than to the mind. Imagination is the only way to talk truthfully about ultimate reality. When talking about God, as Karl Barth noted, we are often perplexed and can't make any sense of it from a human point of view. God acts in ways that transcend human understanding. That's why agnosticism and atheism are rationally appealing. Evil seems to have the upper hand, especially with so much violence and hate in the world. To talk about God in the face of evil seems like nonsense. But faith, transcending reason, says God will not let evil have the last word about the truth of the cross.

The cross is evil (no doubt about that!) but that's not the only thing we can say about it. The cross is also a transcendent transvaluation of values, as Reinhold Niebuhr says in *Beyond Tragedy* (1938). That's what Paul was saying: "God chose what is low and despised in the world, things that are not, to reduce to nothing things that are" (1 Cor 1:28). From a rational point of view, this sounds crazy. Yet, I knew I couldn't stop speaking about the cross, even though I knew that Williams had made a point I couldn't ignore. She was not the only person criticizing the idea of redemptive suffering. White feminists, before Williams, had offered similar criticisms,[11] which probably influenced her. Then Third World feminists joined the chorus.[12] I couldn't turn away from feminist scholars of religion who said the cross contributes to the suffering of poor women, causing them to be passive, like Jesus on the cross, in the face of domestic violence.

My critics were the best thing that ever happened to me as a theologian, even though I didn't think so at the time. Accepting criticism is a hard but necessary lesson to learn. Critics made me think deeper and clearer, never letting me take myself for granted. They kept me on my toes, kept the fire burning over nearly fifty years. Thank God for critics!

The worst thing is to be ignored or to have said nothing worth responding to. Silence kills thought and imagination. I received all kinds of criticism, some worthless and others a blessing. I had to decide what was important and what wasn't.

---

11. See especially the important collection of essays, Joanne Carlson Brown and Carole R. Bohn, eds., *Christianity, Patriarchy and Abuse: A Feminist Critique* (New York: Pilgrim Press, 1989).

12. See Ivone Gebara, *Out of the Depths: Women's Experience of Evil and Salvation* (Minneapolis: Augsburg, 2002).

Appreciation is also important. Like criticism, such appreciation fuels one's passion to work harder—to think deeper and more creatively. Appreciation motivates me to try to write better, with spiritual insight and a bluesy feeling. When I am writing I like to read the classics, especially Toni Morrison and James Baldwin, to remind me what good writing looks like and how to engage suffering in the black community. I know I will never reach their standard, but they keep me humble, reaching for the beauty in language. Whenever someone tells me that I am a good writer or that she or he couldn't put my book down, I'm speechless and don't know what to say in response. It took me years to find my voice and to write with skill and careful attention to detail. Theologians should think about *how* to write and *what* to say. Both are important, especially when writing about black people, who have a style, grace, and beauty in the way they live, which is not easy to capture in words.

Criticism and appreciation are like steroids added to thought and imagination. After womanist criticism, I couldn't stop reading and writing. I kept asking myself, what can I say, especially about Williams? I started teaching a course on "God, Suffering and the Human Being," using all my favorite texts: Gutiérrez's *On Job*, Albert Camus's *The Plague*, Dostoevsky's "The Grand Inquisitor," Toni Morrison's *Beloved*, Chinua Achebe's *Things Fall Apart*, Dorothee Soelle's *Suffering*, Ivone Gebara's *Out of the Depths,* and Victor Frankl's *Man's Search for Meaning*. I didn't find the answer to the problem of suffering but explored many questions about it, which was far more important.

I also taught a course on "Martin Luther King Jr. and Malcolm X" and wrote *Martin & Malcolm & America* (1991), which took ten years of research and writing. It deepened my understanding of black suffering. No one understood black suffering more deeply and fought harder to eliminate it than Martin and Malcolm. No religious figures influenced black liberation theology more than they. But Martin and Malcolm, though important for my wrestling with suffering, were not enough. Then I turned to the master essayist, James Baldwin, who proved to be my most challenging and important interlocutor.

What separates me from Delores Williams and other womanists and feminists who share her perspective is the spiritual depth of Southern black religion that shaped my life in Bearden. At the center of this faith is Jesus's cross, the exodus, and the prophets. While I read many books on suffering, it was the suffering of black people and how they used their faith to resist dehumanization that defined the way I talk and write about these themes. Williams challenged the heart of black faith and pushed me to the brink of denial, but I refused to step over the edge. To do that would have left me with no place to stand. I chose to stand with the community of faith in which I grew up, the community that sang and preached about the "Old Ship of Zion," which "has landed many a thousand." I got on board when I was a child. Black religion has brought many through the storms of life, and the more I dig deep into its meaning, the more I am convicted by it.

Suffering in black life took me to the cross of Jesus and the lynching of African Americans. I couldn't stop thinking about their similarities—historically and religiously. That was why I wrote *The Cross and the Lynching Tree* (2011), which engaged me fully, causing dread and many sleepless nights. I was searching for words to respond to womanist criticism.

CHAPTER 6

I Started Walkin' and Talkin'

The Cross and the Lynching Tree

People often asked me, "Which of your books is your favorite?" I really couldn't say. It's like choosing one of my children—not an easy choice to make, and one we probably shouldn't entertain. But with *The Cross and the Lynching Tree* (2011), my latest offspring, I now have a favorite. It is definitely the most difficult and challenging book I've written, a culmination of my life's work that engaged not only my mind but also the spiritual dimension of my whole being. I put my whole self into it, holding nothing back. As I wrote, I had to wrestle with memories I had wanted to forget, but could not. It's almost as if I didn't choose to write it, but it chose me.

When people ask, "How long did it take you to write *The Cross and the Lynching Tree*?" I realize that the active time was about ten years of research, thinking, and writing. It took many false starts and several drafts before the book reached its published form. I took my time and chose every word carefully, feeling that nothing less than the integrity of black faith and the freedom struggle that arose from it were at stake. Yet, in the deepest sense, I have been writing that book all my life. And I am still writing it. It won't truly be complete until I draw my last breath.

I first sat down to write *The Cross and the Lynching Tree* in the mountains of Colorado, near Aspen, 9,000 feet above sea level, surrounded only by white people. I was reminded of the fear I felt in Southern sundown towns in rural Arkansas. For many months the words would not come. I kept ripping up pages, asking myself why I was writing this book, what did I want to say, and to whom? I wanted to address the redemptive significance of Jesus's cross and black suffering, but I first had to consider the powerful critique of womanist theology, which had arrested my attention for months, and then years. I knew I had no answer for the problem of suffering; I wasn't actually looking for one, since answers only stifle the imagination and cover up the deeper existential questions. I wanted to explore the meaning of Jesus's cross in America, for both black and white Christians. As I reflected on the cross, my mind kept returning to the lynching tree, the most horrific manifestation of black suffering in the United States. I sensed a connection, but didn't know how to articulate it. Frustrated, I meditated deeply on the story of Jesus's crucifixion in the Gospel of Mark but also returned to the work of artists like Baldwin, Toni Morrison, and Richard Wright, hoping they would inspire me. Still, the words came slowly.

In 2006, I accepted an invitation to deliver the Ingersoll Lecture at Harvard Divinity School and proposed the title, "Strange Fruit: The Cross and the Lynching Tree."[1] I was taking a risk, because I hadn't yet written anything and didn't

---

1. See James H. Cone, "Strange Fruit: The Cross and the Lynching Tree," *Harvard Divinity School Bulletin* 35, no. 1 (Winter 2007): 45–55.

know what I would say. I started with the text: "They put him to death by hanging him on a tree" (Acts 10:39)—Peter's powerful depiction of Jesus's crucifixion as a public lynching.

Then I turned to Countee Cullen's poem "Recrucified Christ" (1922), written during the lynching era, when he was only nineteen. Cullen, a Harlem Renaissance poet, who also taught James Baldwin at Frederick Douglass Junior High School, said what I wanted to say: "The South is crucifying Christ again," a gripping, insightful, and obviously truthful religious claim. When whites lynched black people, they were lynching Christ. Why hadn't I said that in my writings as clearly as Cullen wrote it in his short sonnet of just fourteen lines? Black Christians have always believed that Jesus suffered with them, since he suffered as they do. Jesus would know how blacks feel, because he suffered too. Recalling this is how blacks weathered the storm of white supremacy for four hundred years. But I didn't say what Cullen and other black artists said: that Christ was a lynched black body. It wasn't something we talked about in church or preached in sermons. Piety and fear blinded us from seeing Christ's body as a black victim on a hanging tree. Although Cullen was a Methodist minister's son, he wasn't a religious man; perhaps that aided his penetrating insight and the clarity of his language. Cullen wrote:

> Christ's awful wrong is that he's dark of hue,
> The sin for which no blamelessness atones;
> But lest the sameness of the cross should tire
> They kill him now with famished tongues of fire,
> And while he burns, good men, and women, too
> Shout, battling for black and brittle bones.

Cullen stripped away the religious piety and theological jargon that prevented Christians from seeing the plain truth: that the lynching tree was America's cross.

Lastly, I turned to Billie Holiday's haunting rendition of Abel Meeropol's "Strange Fruit."

> Southern trees bear strange fruit,
> Blood on the leaves and blood at the root,
> Black bodies swinging in the southern breeze,
> Strange fruit hanging from the poplar trees.

Holiday, like Cullen, was not a church-going Christian. Nothing prevented her from expressing the feeling of dread that lynching created for black life. I was mesmerized by the sound of her voice as I imagined black bodies swinging from Southern trees.

The mood was set for me to write my lecture and later my book. Although Harvard was a challenging intellectual context, I wasn't thinking about that. Instead, I was thinking about Peter's sermon, Cullen's poem, and Holiday's song, and what they could tell me about the meaning of the cross and the lynching tree in the United States. Starting to write became a transforming experience, and I found myself saying things with clarity and a power that surprised me.

The Cross and the Lynching Tree engaged my mind, heart, and soul like no other subject. For years, I had been wrestling with the great paradox of black suffering and the Christian gospel—talking about it in books and essays, in my classes at Union, in lectures and sermons across the country and around the world. But the lynching tree deepened the paradox, and made faith especially difficult.

Shortly after the Harvard lecture, I received a call from the office of Bill Moyers, who invited me to have a conversation about the cross and the lynching tree that would be broadcast to the nation on his public television program, "Bill Moyers Journal." I hesitated; I don't like appearing on television. Besides, I still had a lot of research and thinking to do. My book was five years away from being finished. Then Moyers himself called to talk about his hope to interview me soon. "We need you to talk to the nation about lynching and the cross," he said, "and relate it to what's happening in Jenna, Louisiana"—referring to an incident that was all over the news. In a schoolyard in Jenna three nooses had been found hanging from a tree in a schoolyard, creating much tension and rage and provoking altercations between black and white students. The Jenna Six were six black teenagers who were initially charged with attempted second-degree murder for beating a white student. The charge was obviously racially motivated, and it was later reduced to simple battery, following a public outcry.

Before long, nooses were appearing all over the United States—both South and North—in work places and police stations, colleges, and universities. One noose appeared across the street from me at Columbia Teachers College. It reminded me of when I first arrived at Union and someone in the seminary community changed the name on my office door from "Dr. Cone" to "Dr. Coon." I said nothing to no one; the name change was soon corrected, and nothing like that ever happened again.

I wasn't sure whether I could explain to an audience of mostly white people what the cross and the lynching tree meant for me and for American Christians. But I decided to try, largely because of my respect for Bill Moyers. It was the fall of 2007, and Barack Obama was about to be elected America's first African American president. It was a time of hope and change and "Yes, We Can." But the nooses sent another message: "Not so fast!"

In the process of that conversation with Moyers,[2] I realized what I wanted to say to America: that the lynchers didn't have the last word about black humanity. That is the redemptive significance of black resistance. We are still here, still resisting. As long as black people fight back, our resistance redeems the lynching tree. The Emmett Till lynching in Money, Mississippi, ignited the civil rights movement, and the murder of four girls in a Birmingham church, two weeks after the March on Washington, aroused a determined black community throughout the United States to fight against white supremacy until freedom comes.

The question that preoccupied me is this: How did African Americans *survive* and *resist* the lynching terror, while maintaining enough sanity to love each other and marry, raise their children, and teach them love and respect? Faith in God and in themselves is what kept many blacks emotionally and spiritually healthy enough to love not only themselves but also to reject hatred. Mississippi Freedom fighter Fannie Lou Hamer was right: "Only God has kept the Negro sane."[3] Whites often used Christianity to justify

---

2. See Bill Moyers, *Bill Moyers Journal: The Conversation Continues* (New York: New Press, 2011), 316–27. See also the broadcast available on YouTube and the Harvard Lecture www.hds.havard.edu/news/events_online/igersoll_2006.html.

3. Cited in David Chappell, *A Stone of Hope: Prophetic Religion and the Death of Jim Crow* (Chapel Hill: University of North Carolina Press, 2004), 74.

the lynching of blacks, while blacks found in Christianity the resources to survive and resist.

The more I reflected on the cross and the lynching tree the more I understood why black Christians could not turn away from the cross, even though that symbol was used to enslave, segregate, and lynch them. The cross did not make black suffering easier to bear, but it enabled some people to survive it. That is the great paradox in black life. We can't solve this dilemma. It is a great wound we have to live with. The cross is a part of the Christian condition, so long as the world remains unredeemed. It is the answer to oppressed people who struggle for liberation. It remains at the center of the gospel of Jesus, and it remains at the center of black life in the United States, in the form of the lynching tree.

I have spent a lifetime pointing out the hypocrisy and mendacity of the white church in a white-dominated society, and at the same time raising up and exalting the voices and experiences of the oppressed. I write out of my experience as an African American growing up in segregated Arkansas and out of a deep theological conviction that the true power of the Christian gospel lies in its clear call for liberation of the oppressed and a fierce condemnation of their oppressors.

I write on behalf of all those whom the Salvadoran theologian and martyr Ignacio Ellacuría called "the crucified peoples of history." I write for the forgotten and the abused, the marginalized and the despised. I write for those who are penniless, jobless, landless, all those who have no political or social power. I write for gays, lesbians, bisexuals, and those who are transgender. I write for immigrants stranded on the U.S. border and for undocumented farmworkers toiling in misery in the nation's agricultural fields. I write for

Palestinians in the Gaza Strip, on the West Bank, and in East Jerusalem. I write for Muslims and refugees who live under the terror of war in Iraq, Afghanistan, and Syria. And I write for all people who care about humanity. I believe that until Americans, especially Christians and theologians, can see the cross and the lynching tree together, until we can identify Christ with "recrucified" black bodies hanging from lynching trees, there can be no genuine understanding of Christian identity in America, and no deliverance from the brutal legacy of slavery and white supremacy.

As I started reading about the historical practice of crucifixion in Rome during the time of Jesus, and then about lynching, I was even more struck by the analogy between them. The cross was not just a form of execution; it was an instrument of terror, intended as a warning to anyone who would challenge the power of Rome. In the same way, the lynching tree was not just a terrible punishment inflicted on its victims; it sent a warning to all black people, demonstrating the power of white supremacy, which could strike anyone with impunity and at any time. Nearly five thousand African American men, women, and children were lynched in America following the Civil War, and their devastated families were left behind to cope with their great loss—fathers and mothers, brothers and sisters, uncles and aunts, nephews and nieces, cousins and friends and other loved ones strung up on trees and burned beyond recognition, their body parts often distributed as souvenirs. But the message was directed to all black people; none were exempt from the horror of the lynching tree.

To live under the terror of death was no easy matter. Having grown up in Arkansas, I knew from experience something about lynching. I watched my mother and father deal with the memory and threats of lynching, a topic they discussed with their three sons. But as I read more about it, examining the historical records, listening daily to Billie Holiday sing "Strange Fruit," reading James Baldwin's words about "those photographs of Negroes hanged from trees,"[4] "blood dripping down through leaves, gouged-out eyeballs, the sex torn from its socket and severed with a knife,"[5] I could not stop thinking that I might have been one of those "black bodies swinging in the Southern breeze." My father and brothers and even my mother could have been "strange fruit hanging from the poplar trees." It was a horrifying nightmare to think and dream about.

"How many times," Baldwin writes, "has the southern day come up to find a black man, sexless, hanging from a tree?"[6] It shook me at the core of my being, disrupting my Christian identity, and making *The Cross and the Lynching Tree* the most painful book I have written, from a "pain so old and deep and black."[7] The horror of lynching is in my blood, flowing throughout my body. The images of lynching appeared in my dreams. And yet, strange and paradoxical as it may appear, I discovered that it was black people's identification with the cross on which Jesus was brutally crucified that kept many of them out of a madhouse. That was why they sang with passion, "Jesus, Keep Me Near the Cross." It was their faith in

---

4. James Baldwin, "A Fly in Buttermilk," in *Collected Essays*, ed. Toni Morrison (New York: Library of America, 1998), 187.

5. Baldwin, "Alas, Poor Richard," in *Collected Essays*, 266.

6. Baldwin, "Nobody Knows My Name: A Letter from the South," in *Collected Essays*, 204.

7. Baldwin, "Down at the Cross," in *Collected Essays*, 323.

Jesus's cross, believing that if God was with Jesus, God must be with us, because we are also on the cross.

But there was another question to ponder: How could white Christians, who also claim to believe that Jesus died on the cross to save them, then turn around and put blacks on trees and kill them? That was an amazing paradox: two communities, both Christian, embracing the same faith. Whites even lynched people on church grounds. How could they do it?

Part of the answer lay in the unfortunate fact, during the course of two thousand years of Christian history, that the cross as a symbol of salvation had been detached from the ongoing suffering and oppression of human beings, the crucified people of history. The cross was transformed into a harmless, nonoffensive ornament that Christians wear around their necks. Rather than reminding us of the cost of discipleship, it became a form of "cheap grace," as the German theologian and martyr Dietrich Bonhoeffer put it—an easy way to claim salvation without confronting the power of Christ's message and mission.

In my chapter on Reinhold Niebuhr, America's most important Christian social ethicist of the twentieth century, I expose Niebuhr's blindness to black oppression and his tacit complicity with it. Slavery, segregation, and lynching find little or no place in Niebuhr's theological reflections, or that of any other white theologian. Niebuhr had little empathy for the "lesser" races subjugated by white colonialists. He claimed that North America was a virgin continent when the Anglo-Saxons came, with a few Indians in a primitive state of culture. Niebuhr saw America as divinely destined to expand into an empire, and he wrote about Arabs of Palestine and people of color in the Third World in the same way as he wrote about Indians, offering moral justification for colonialism.

In a radio dialogue between Niebuhr and James Baldwin following the September 1963 bombing of the Sixteenth Street Baptist Church in Birmingham that killed four little girls, Niebuhr infuriated Baldwin by speaking of moderation. Baldwin said:

> The only people in this country at the moment who believe either in Christianity or in the country are the most despised minority in it. . . . It is ironical . . . the people who were slaves here, the most beaten and despised people here . . . should be at this moment . . . the only hope this country has. It doesn't have any other. None of the descendants of Europe seem to be able to do, or have taken it on themselves to do what Negroes are now trying to do. And this is not a chauvinistic or racial outlook. It probably has something to do with the nature of life itself. It forces you, in any extremity, any extreme, to discover what you really live by, whereas most Americans have been for so long, so safe and so sleepy, that they don't any longer have any real sense of what they live by. I think they really think it may be Coca-Cola.[8]

Michelle Alexander shows that the same thing is happening today in the prison industrial complex, which she calls "the New Jim Crow."[9] There is more than one way of lynch-

---

8. Cited in James H. Cone, *The Cross and the Lynching Tree* (Maryknoll, NY: Orbis Books, 2011), 54.
9. Michelle Alexander, *The New Jim Crow* (New York: New Press, 2012).

arcerate them and shoot them down
streets of our cities. The murders of
Charleston, South Carolina, Alton Ster-
ɔuge, Louisiana, Philando Castile (2016)
ta, and many more black men, women,
ne face of lynching in twenty-first century
re many other names we don't know. How
ı Americans have to live under the terror of
y?

ʋas Martin Luther King Jr.'s answer to that
address following the March from Selma to
i966).[10] "How long will justice be crucified,
r it? . . . How long? Not long, because the arc of
the m∪⌐ ∪iverse is long, but it bends toward justice." But
a few years later, he was near despair over the escalation of
America's involvement in the Vietnam War, the deepening
of poverty, and the endurance of white supremacy. Sound-
ing like a nonviolent Malcolm X, he lamented, "They are
turning my dream into a nightmare."

In writing *The Cross and the Lynching Tree*, I found my
inspiration in the faith of black people and in militant black
ministers like Martin Luther King Jr. and Malcolm X, activists like Ida B. Wells and Fannie Lou Hamer, and writers
such as James Baldwin, Toni Morrison, and Richard Wright,
along with the great blues artists of my youth. These ministers, activists, and artists gave me a sense of awe in the
presence of humanity, fighting for justice against great odds.

---

10. For King's address "Our God Is Marching On!" see *A Testament
of Hope: The Essential Writings of Martin Luther King, Jr.*, ed. James M.
Washington (New York: Harper & Row, 1986), 227–30.

I saw that for most ordinary blacks, it was their music and their faith that offered them the chief weapons of resistance. In the words of poets and writers, in blues singers, and in the thunderous services of the black church, many were able to confront the bleak circumstances of their lives and yet defy fate and suffering and make the most of what life had offered them. Through these connections, I found a way to respond to black suffering in all of its forms.

Being a Christian is somewhat like being black. It's a paradox, a profound contradiction, with many incongruities. You grow up black, and you can't help but wonder why whites treat you as though you were not a human being. It is hard to figure that out, especially as a child. At the same time, my mother and father would tell me, "Don't hate like they hate," for as James Baldwin wrote, "Hatred [is] too heavy a sack to carry."[11] It was my parents' faith that gave them the inner resources to transcend the brutality and see the real beauty in the tragedy of their lives. It is a mystery, a profound and deep mystery, how many African Americans, even after two and half centuries of slavery and another century of lynching and Jim Crow segregation, still refuse to allow themselves to be infected with hatred. Nothing illustrated this more than the families of the "Emanuel Nine," the black Christians who were murdered in Charleston, South Carolina, as they attended a Bible study in their church. Their families offered forgiveness to the young white man, Dylan Roof, who had so coldly shot their loved ones. That was a profound religious achievement.

---

11. Baldwin, "The Fire Next Time," in *Collected Essays*, 343.

Many whites, and blacks too, were baffled by this offer of forgiveness. To many it seemed grossly out of place from a human point of view. But forgiveness is not weakness or passivity. It is spiritual resistance, a revolt against hatred, the refusal to allow the hater to make you like him, which is what Dylan Roof wanted. "You become what you hate,"[12] Baldwin rightly said. But "it demands great spiritual resilience not to hate the hater. . . ."[13] Jesus set the example from the cross. His words, "Father, forgive them, for they do not know what they are doing" (Luke 23:34), empowered black Christians to do the same. That was why Martin Luther King Jr. preached and lived nonviolence, which was love resisting white supremacy. King created the most transformative social movement in American history based on love and forgiveness, derived from his faith in Jesus's cross. Jesus's cry from the cross, "Father, into your hands I commend my spirit" (Luke 23:46) confirmed what he said in the Gospel of Matthew: "Do not fear people who can kill the body. They cannot kill the spirit" (10:28). The Black Spirit of resistance cannot be destroyed by white supremacy. It is a transcendent force rooted in black history and found today among the relatives of the Emanuel Nine, in the Black Lives Matter movement, and even among black National Football League players taking a knee during the national anthem to protest the killing of black people in the streets of America.

The cross is a paradoxical religious symbol because it *inverts* the world's value system, proclaiming that hope comes

---

12. Baldwin, *Conversations*, 238.
13. Baldwin, "The Fire Next Time," 343.

by way of defeat, that suffering and death do not have the last word, that the last shall be first and the first last. Secular intellectuals find this idea absurd, but it is profoundly real in the spiritual life of black folk. For many who were tortured and lynched, the crucified Christ often manifested God's loving and liberating presence *within* the great contradictions of black life. The cross of Jesus is what empowered black Christians to believe, ultimately, that they would not be defeated by the "troubles of the world," no matter how great and painful their suffering. Only people stripped of power could understand this absurd claim of faith. The cross was God's critique of power—white power—with powerless love, snatching victory from the jaws of defeat.

Present-day Christians misinterpret the cross when they make it a nonoffensive religious symbol, a decorative object in their homes and churches. The cross, therefore, needs the lynching tree to remind us what it means when we say that God is revealed in Jesus at Golgotha, the place of the skull, on the cross where criminals and rebels against the Roman state were executed. The lynching tree is America's cross. What happened to Jesus in Jerusalem happened to blacks in Arkansas, Mississippi, and Kentucky. Lynched black bodies are symbols of Christ's body. If we want to understand what the crucifixion means for Americans today, we must view it through the lens of mutilated black bodies whose lives are destroyed in the criminal justice system. Jesus continues to be lynched before our eyes. He is crucified wherever people are tormented. That is why I say Christ is black.

The power of the cross is difficult to articulate adequately; but when one lives it, its truth is self-evident. I have seen the transforming power of faith in the cross among many black

Christians who struggle for right, especially among freedom fighters in the civil rights movement. Knowing they could be killed at any time, many wrote their wills. They knew they were enemies of the state and were not going to win with guns and tanks. But they did what they did because the transcendent reality they encountered in that justice moment was more powerful than the opposition.

They needed the power of that belief to overcome what James Baldwin called his "worst discovery: . . . not only that society treated me like a *nigger* and thought of me as one, but that I *myself* believed it—that I *believed* what white people said of me." He said it took "many years of vomiting up all the filth I had been taught about myself . . . before I was able to walk on earth as though I had a right to be here."[14]

Unlike Baldwin and many blacks, I don't remember wishing that I was white. Being black in Bearden at Macedonia AME Church seemed to me so beautiful, as I saw blackness embodied in the lives of my mother and father and a host of other proud men and women in Arkansas. The reality of love in my own community was so strong, so real, that I truly loved being black. The spiritual values of my parents and other blacks were more important than the material things I saw in the white world that hated me. Black music and dance, black loving, hugging, and kissing, black preaching and singing—everything black seemed much more interesting and inspiring.

The beauty of blackness was everywhere: from Joe Louis knocking out Max Schmeling with power and grace to Jesse

---

14. Cited in Fern Marja Eckman, *The Furious Passage of James Baldwin* (New York: M. Evans, 1966), 79, 154.

Owens running with pride for his 〔   〕 ce of
Hitler's hate and German white supren〔   〕 son
and Willie Mays hitting balls, running〔   〕 d-
ing, making art on a baseball diamond. 〔   〕
make art out of anything, put their black s〔   〕
they did, like Goose Tatum and Marques H〔   〕
lem Globetrotters shooting and dribbling, er〔   〕
ple around the world with a basketball, amazi〔   〕
and so black. There was so much to love about〔   〕
whether in the juke joint or at the dance hall, bl〔   〕
were swinging and moving to the blues sound of 〔   〕
and Muddy Waters, or in the church listening to th〔   〕
of Sister Ora Wallace singing "I'm working on a buildi〔   〕
my mother, Lucy Cone, raising her voice, proclaiming, 〔_〕ns
little light of mine." Black beauty was all over Bearden, in the
laughter and play, the style of black talk and walk. As a child
I was in my element; blackness kept me sane, believing that
I was somebody.

Although I learned to wear a mask in Arkansas and in
graduate school, for the last fifty-something years I've tried
to remove that mask, and to encourage other African Americans to do the same: to stop acting, to get in touch with that
inner resource that frees them to speak as clearly, forcefully,
and as truthfully as they can.

I have felt deeply the need to write for people who have
no voice, for those people, as Martin Luther King Jr. said,
"who have been left out of the sunlight of opportunity." If
there was passion in what I wrote, that's because I was trying
to do justice to the faith and courage of African Americans
who survived and resisted slavery, Jim Crow segregation,
and lynching. I wanted to bear witness as best I could to the

black blood *still* flowing in the streets, jails, and even in our churches and all the byways of America.

"Writing is a form of prayer," Franz Kafka wrote in his diary. *The Cross and the Lynching Tree* is my prayer, my invocation to God on behalf of black people in the hope that their nearly four centuries of suffering will be redemptive for our children and grandchildren, revealing to them the beauty in their tragic past, and thereby empowering them to fight the violence of white supremacy. "Black Lives Matter" is a partial realization of my hope. It is also my hope that whites, too, will be redeemed from their blindness and open their eyes to the terror of their deeds so they will know that we are all of one blood, brothers and sisters, literally and symbolically, and that what they do to blacks, they do to themselves.

Let us hope, through God's grace and our struggle together, that we will be able to overcome our prejudices and the hate that separates us, and thereby empower people of all races and faiths to become the one people God created us to be.

CHAPTER 7

I Started Singin' and Shoutin'

Learning from Baldwin

"If [God's] love was so great," wrote James Baldwin, "and if He loved all His children, why are we, the blacks, cast down so far?"[1]—a straightforward question that anyone can understand, asked by one of the great prophets in the twentieth century, one hundred years after the Emancipation Proclamation. I've asked the same question all my life and still have no answer. "What's going on?" That was the question soul musician Marvin Gaye rightly asked about the Vietnam War and the social unrest in the United States, and it's still relevant today!

> Mother, mother
> There's too many of you crying
> Brother, brother, brother
> There's too many of you dying

"Makes me want to holler," *What's going on*? How long, Lord, will we have to ask?

---

1. James Baldwin, "The Fire Next Time," in *Collected Essays*, ed. Toni Morrison (New York: Library of America, 1998), 304.

Like me, James Baldwin was brought up to be a preacher who understood something about the black religious experience. No one can read *Go Tell It on the Mountain* and not know that for James Baldwin God was real. He had been on "the threshing floor" all night, "passed through the fire,"[2] as the saints prayed him through, got up and left God's house to preach the gospel of love to the world, which he couldn't do in the church. It was too hypocritical and too absorbed with its own holiness, unable to see beyond its own piety. Baldwin left the church as Jesus left the temple, and, like Jesus, embraced sinners, prostitutes, outcasts, and felons. "What Christians seem not to do," he told Margaret Mead, "is identify with the man they call their Savior, who, after all, was a very disreputable person when he was alive and who was put to death by Rome. . . . Everyone forgets that."[3]

But Baldwin did not forget. He wrote about the "disreputable Hebrew criminal" in essays and books and talked about him at the World Council of Churches (WCC) Assembly, when he took the place of Martin Luther King Jr., who had been assassinated three months earlier.[4] "The whole question . . . of religion has always really obsessed me," he told Mead. "So, in my case, in order to become a moral human being, whatever that may be, I have to hang out with publicans and sinners, whores and junkies, and stay out of the temple where they told us nothing but lies anyway." In

2. James Baldwin, "The Devil Finds Work," in *Collected Essays,* 565.

3. Margaret Mead and James Baldwin, *A Rap on Race* (New York: Dell, 1971), 89.

4. James Baldwin, "White Racism or World Community" (July 7, 1968), in *Collected Essays,* 749–56. Baldwin's address was first published in *The Ecumenical Review,* October 20, 1968.

agreement, Mead remarked, "This is, of course, what Jesus did too." "Yes," Baldwin replied, "it is only in this sense that I can be called a Christian."[5]

Lies and self-hatred drove Baldwin out of the church; and lies and self-hatred placed me on its margins. Searching for answers to the problem of black suffering that I could not find in either church or in theology, I started to read Baldwin and couldn't stop. I was captivated by his eloquence and religious insights about that "sun-baked" "criminal Jew"[6] from Galilee and his relentless and devastating criticism of the Christian church. He spoke to me like no other writer.

James Arthur Baldwin was born August 2, 1924, in New York's Harlem Hospital, one year before Malcolm X and five prior to Martin Luther King Jr. He was, as Mumia Abu-Jamal said, a "word warrior"[7] for justice. In his eulogy, Amiri Baraka called him "God's black revolutionary mouth."[8] His biographer, W. J. Weatherby, referred to him as an "artist on fire."[9] Baldwin's book-length essay "The Fire Next Time," which one writer called "the literary equivalent of Malcolm X,"[10] sold over one million copies and was selected by the Library of Congress as one of the eighty-eight books that shook

5. Mead and Baldwin, *A Rap on Race,* 86, 89.

6. See Baldwin, "The Fire Next Time," 312, and "White Racism and World Community," 755.

7. Mumia Abu-Jamal, "James Baldwin: Word Warrior," Prison Radio, July 17, 2017.

8. Amiri Baraka, "Jimmy," in *James Baldwin: The Legacy,* ed. Quincy Troupe (New York: Simon & Schuster/Touchstone, 1989), 134.

9. W. J. Weatherby, *James Baldwin: Artist on Fire* (New York: Dutton, 1990).

10. See Carol Polsgrove, *Divided Minds: Intellectuals and the Civil Rights Movement* (New York: W. W. Norton, 2001), 164.

America. (Malcolm X's *Autobiography* was also selected.) If one reads only one book by James Baldwin this is the one. It is a sermon to America—first appearing in *The New Yorker* with the title, "Letter from a Region in My Mind" (November 1962) and later published as a book, along with "A Letter to My Nephew," which also made a prior appearance in *The Progressive* (December 1962). In these essays he wrestles with God, suffering, and America.

Baldwin ends his epistle asking for the impossible, which he said was "the least that one can demand."[11] The times are urgent. Judgment is upon America. "The relatively conscious whites and the relatively conscious blacks . . . must, like lovers, insist on, or create the consciousness of others. . . . If we do not falter in our duty now," he writes, "we may be able, handful that we are, to end the racial nightmare." Seeing what Baldwin saw coming, it would have been "easy to be bleak about the human race." But his faith in humanity would not let him despair. "Despair is sin," he said, soon after "Fire Next Time" was published. His hope for America, for blacks and whites and humanity, was not optimism. It was a tough hope, hope in the midst of the coming nightmare. Baldwin saw himself as "a kind of Jeremiah,"[12] prophesying an imminent destruction, which his people don't want to hear. Baldwin was writing in 1962, before the urban fires (Birmingham, Watts, New York, Newark, and Detroit) that swept through America's cities. Americans could not say they were not warned. "If we do not now dare everything,"

---

11. Baldwin, "The Fire Next Time," 346.
12. See Baldwin, "The American and the American Negro" in *Collected Essays*, 714.

he pleaded, "the fulfillment of the prophecy, re-created from the Bible in song by a slave, is upon us: *God gave Noah the rainbow sign, no more water, but the fire next time!*"[13]

Just as ancient Israel ignored the prophecy of Jeremiah, so America ignored Baldwin. A striking exception was the Trappist monk Thomas Merton, a major white religious writer. "You are right all down the line," Merton said in a letter to Baldwin, later published in *Seeds of Destruction*. "You exaggerate nowhere. You know exactly what you are talking about...." Merton correctly saw the religious character of "Fire Next Time." "I think your view is fundamentally religious, and therefore has to be against conventional religiosity."[14] Not everyone agreed with Merton about Baldwin's "Fire." Martin E. Marty, a prominent religious historian, objected strongly to Merton's scathing critique of the "white liberal" and his prophecy of violence in *Seeds of Destruction*. "Merton seems to be imitating the style and mood of James Baldwin . . . who has read a great deal of history wrong," he wrote. But, three years later, following the Newark and Detroit rebellions, Marty was forced to change his mind. In an apology to Merton, he wrote him, "Now it seems to me you were 'telling it as it is,'" and not "trying to be a kind of white James Baldwin."[15]

Reflecting on the urban fires in July 1967, during which

---

13. Baldwin, "The Fire Next Time," 347.

14. Thomas Merton, *Seeds of Destruction* (New York: Farrar, Straus & Giroux, 1964).

15. Martin Marty, "Sowing Thorns in the Flesh," *The Sunday Tribune*, January 17, 1965; Martin Marty, "To: Thomas Merton. Re: Your Prophecy," August 30, 1967, *The National Catholic Reporter*, August 30, 1967.

twenty-seven people were killed in Newark and forty-three in Detroit, I picked up Baldwin's "Fire" again, as I wrestled with the fire burning hot inside me. I also read again the *Autobiography of Malcolm X.* He had been called the angriest Negro in America, and he spoke to the blackness and rage seeking expression inside me. I was the angriest black theologian in America! I had heard Martin King's preaching become inflamed with passion about the Christian gospel of love, which spoke to my Christian identity and made irrelevant everything I had read on the subject in graduate school. But how could I write with the fire of blackness like Malcolm and the passion of love like Martin? I found the answer in James Baldwin. I saw in Baldwin what I liked in Martin and Malcolm—blackness and love, defined by justice for all and a vision of hope in the face of the enduring power and absurdity of white supremacy. No wonder Negroes had to create the blues, and no one could articulate their meaning like Baldwin. "It is simply impossible not to sing the blues . . . when the lives lived by Negroes are so inescapably harsh and stunted."[16] Reading Baldwin helped me sing my theological blues in *Black Theology and Black Power*, as I struggled to make sense out of the urban disasters in the 1960s. The blues come out of all of that.

Baldwin's insight about suffering gave me back to the black folk religion that had nurtured and kept me alive during my childhood in Arkansas. In seminary I had grown ashamed of my religious roots, turning instead to European theologians like Barth, Tillich, and Niebuhr. But they were

---

16. Baldwin, "The Harlem Ghetto," in "Notes of a Native Son," in *Collected Essays*, 47.

not my heritage. They took me away from my source and I was never truly at home with them. They didn't speak to the existential pain I felt or the suffering I inherited.

The Detroit uprising shook the foundation of my being. And then King's assassination, eight months later, drove me crazy with rage. Reading white theology, I thought of the words of the African artist Chinua Achebe: "just another piece of deodorized dog shit." Reflecting on the European idea of "art for art's sake," he had noted: "Literature is not a luxury for us. It is a life and death affair because we are fashioning a new [humanity]."[17] That's what black theology was for me, and I embraced Baldwin as my theological mentor.

In 2011, I was invited to speak about James Baldwin at the Cathedral Church of Saint John the Divine, to mark his induction into The Poet's Corner. Not knowing where to begin, I said: "There is so much that he has given to us—to young and old people, blacks and whites, people of all races and nationalities, genders and sexual orientations, not only in America but also throughout the world. He offers something for everyone. We could speak of his legacy as one of America's greatest prose writers in the twentieth century, or as an influential novelist and playwright. . . . People who read him become better human beings, moved by his insight, and his care and love for others."

Many people now are reading Baldwin's work with new interest. His influence seems to be everywhere—even on a U.S. postage stamp. His books and essays are taught in public schools, colleges, and seminary classrooms. People talk

---

17. Cited in Ruth Franklin, "After Empire: Chinua Achebe and the Great African Novel," *The New Yorker*, May 26, 2008.

about him in churches and on the streets. Raoul Peck's Oscar-nominated documentary, "I Am Not Your Negro," "shaped by Baldwin's words" and narrated by the actor Samuel L. Jackson, was widely viewed, stimulating much talk about race. But Baldwin's work is not a comfortable subject; he often speaks sharply, calling white people "moral monsters."[18] He writes, "The brutality with which Negroes are treated in this country simply cannot be overstated, however unwilling white [people] may be to hear it. . . . For the horror of the American Negro's life there has been almost no language. . . . White Americans are probably the sickest and certainly the most dangerous people, of any color, to be found in the world today."[19] Many whites are shocked by such words and object to having their children reading Baldwin in school.

Since I'm neither a professor nor a writer of literature, I initially hesitated when I thought about teaching a course on Baldwin's life and writings. But because I was wrestling with black suffering and criticism of the cross, I needed his work to engage those topics with my students. What could I say that would deepen their ethical commitment to justice as they prepared for ministry? I knew that what scholars wrote about him often snuffed out the fire I loved in his work. Yet as a theologian, an interpreter of the religious imagination of black people, I felt I had much to say. I was not troubled by the fact that Baldwin, after starting to preach at fourteen, had left the pulpit three years later to become a writer who sharply criticized the church. He wrote, "It is not too much to say that

---

18. See especially "I Am Not Your Negro," in "No Name in the Street," in *Collected Essays*, 386; also "Notes of a Native Son," in *Collected Essays*, 129.

19. Baldwin, "The Fire Next Time," 326.

whoever wishes to become a moral human being . . . must first divorce himself from all the prohibitions, crimes, and hypocrisies of the Christian church." Or on another occasion: "If one believes in the Prince of Peace one must stop committing crimes in the name of the Prince of Peace."[20] Speaking to a *New York Times* reporter, who suggested that he was "expressing a religious sentiment" in his writings, Baldwin said, "Every artist is fundamentally religious." Yet he himself had "abandoned Christianity as an organized religion. The church is the worst place to learn about Christianity. I have rejected it because the Christians have rejected Christianity. It is too pious and too hypocritical."[21] To all that I said, "Amen!" Who could blame him for leaving a community that professes beliefs its members don't live by? It was Baldwin's religious rebellion, in fact, that attracted me to him.

One of Baldwin's great insights about suffering is what a Harlem teacher taught him: "that I didn't have to be entirely defined by my circumstances." In an interview with the African American psychologist Kenneth Clark, he said of this teacher that "she was a proof. She was a living proof that I was not necessarily what the country said I was."[22] Baldwin not only heard the message, he passed it on, communicating it in writings around the world, since people of all races, genders, differently abled, and of different sexual orientations needed to know they could transcend their circumstances. If people believe that message and internalize

---

20. Ibid., 314, 756.

21. M. S. Handler, "James Baldwin Rejects Despair Despite Race 'Drift and Danger,'" *New York Times*, June 3, 1963, 1, 19.

22. Kenneth B. Clark, *King, Malcolm, Baldwin: Three Interviews* (Middletown, CT: Wesleyan University Press, 1985), 55.

it, they may overcome their suffering and become more than what others think them to be.

In his classic letter to his nephew, Baldwin wrote, "You can only be destroyed by believing that you really are what the white world calls a *nigger*."[23] He reminded us that Jesus, too, was despised by many people—"put to death by Rome between two thieves, because he claimed to be the Son of God. That claim was a revelation and a revolution because it means we are all sons of God." Baldwin's insight is profoundly theological. It means, he continued, "one can begin to expand and transform God's nature which has to be forever an act of creation on the part of every human being. . . . We are responsible for our soul's salvation . . . ," and ultimately it is our responsibility alone before our "own gods" to deal with our own "health and sickness," "life and death."[24] Mississippian bluesman John Hurt and the Gospel Angelic Singers expressed Baldwin's message as blues and gospel:

> You got to walk that lonesome valley,
> You got to walk it for yourself,
> Ain't nobody to walk it for you,
> You got to walk it for yourself.

"If the concept of God has any validity or any use," Baldwin wrote in "Fire," "it can only make us larger, freer, and more loving. If God cannot do this, then it is time we got rid of Him."[25] After calling Richard Nixon "a motherfucker," thereby shocking everyone at the Cathedral of St. John Divine (1974), which was honoring him as "the artist as prophet," he said,

---

23. Baldwin, "The Fire Next Time," 291.
24. Baldwin, "White Racism and World Community," 755, 756.
25. Baldwin, "The Fire Next Time," 314.

"It's time to think about the Messiah in a new way." It is "time to learn to love each other. The love of God means responsibility to each other."[26] Baldwin was drawing his insights from the black religious experience whose God is "awesome," as the gospel song[27] says, and not to be played with.

"God, after all, is not anybody's toy," Baldwin told an audience at Kalamazoo College. "To be with God is to be involved with some enormous, overwhelming desire, and joy, and power which you cannot control, which controls you. I conceive of my own life as a journey toward something I do not understand, which in going forward, makes me better. I conceive of God, in fact, as a means of *liberation*, and not as a means to control others."[28] For Baldwin, to know God is to struggle with "something out there,"[29] to be "confronted with the agony and nakedness and the beauty of a power which has no beginning and no end, which contains you, and which you contain, and which will be using you when your bones are dust."[30]

Yet as Baldwin shows in *Go Tell It on the Mountain*, not all blacks called on Jesus in the storms of life—a dark, lonesome, and dangerous road with never-ending mental and physical brutality. His character Frank, who didn't know Jesus and didn't want to, spoke for those who "sang the blues and . . . drank too much." "Me and the Lord don't always get along

26. Cited in David Leeming, *James Baldwin: A Biography* (New York: Henry Holt, 1994), 322.

27. "My God Is Awesome," by Pastor Charles Jenkins of Fellowship Baptist Church in Chicago.

28. Baldwin, "In Search of a Majority" (1960), in *Collected Essays*, 220. Emphasis mine.

29. Cited in Leeming, *James Baldwin*, 384.

30. Baldwin, "The Devil Finds Work," 566.

well," he said. "He's running the world like He thinks I ain't got good sense."[31] Others could be harsher, like Richard, also in *Mountain*, who, along with his friends, curses God in "speech," "life," and "heart." When his friend Elizabeth "timidly mentioned the love of Jesus," he reacted derisively, "You can tell that puking bastard to kiss my big black ass."[32]

Baldwin left the church to be with people who didn't go to church. They talked straight and often reacted with anger over any suggestion of insult. They were not to be messed with, and church people knew it. To those who yearned for Africa and remembered High John the Conqueror and prayed to their ancestors, Baldwin said, "I was a . . . bastard of the West" and "an interloper from Africa,"[33] but one who knew that Africa wasn't his home; wherever he traveled, he was an American. Yet Baldwin deepened his solidarity with Africa and its mysteries when he visited the continent; often, Africans thought he was one of them. Other Negroes told stories about Br'er Rabbit and other folkloric tales of how the weak best the strong. Humor was used as a means of survival—"laughing at what he doesn't have that he knows he ought to have,"[34] "laughing to keep from crying."[35] Negroes stayed sane by telling the truth about their experience in a ✓

---

31. James Baldwin, *Go Tell It on the Mountain* (New York: Doubleday, 1952), 77, 78.

32. Ibid., 158.

33. Baldwin, "Notes of a Native Son," 7; and in W. J. Weatherby, *Baldwin*, 176.

34. J. Mason Brewer, "Introduction," in Henry D. Spalding, *Encyclopedia of Black Folklore and Humor* (Middle Village, NY: Jonathan David, 1972), xiii.

35. Langston Hughes, *Laughing to Keep from Crying* (New York: Aeonian Press, 1952).

funny way. "There's always something a little funny in all our disasters," writes Baldwin, "if one can face the disaster."[36] Still others turned to the blues, especially during the lynching era and the reign of Jim Crow segregation.

Baldwin understood the blues feeling, even though, as he said, it was "very hard to describe." It took him back to his beginnings when he was ashamed of his origins, determined to "never touch watermelon,"[37] remembering that his father called him "the ugliest boy he had ever seen."[38] But Bessie Smith, called the Empress of the Blues, helped Baldwin deal with that demeaning description. "I ain't good looking, but I'm somebody's angel child." From his exile in Paris, where he was having difficulty writing *Mountain*, he journeyed to a Swiss village, "armed with two Bessie Smith records and a typewriter." "It was Bessie Smith," he writes, "through her tone and cadence, who helped me to dig back to the way I myself must have spoken when I was a pickaninny, and to remember the things I had heard and seen and felt."[39] Every day he played "Backwater Blues" (1927):

> When it thunders and lightning and the wind
>   begins to blow,
> When it thunders and lightning and the wind
>   begins to blow,

36. James Baldwin, "The Uses of the Blues" (1964), in *The Cross of Redemption: Uncollected Writings*, ed. Randall Kenan (New York: Pantheon, 2010), 59.

37. Studs Terkel, "An Interview with James Baldwin," in *James Baldwin, Conversations with James Baldwin*, ed. Fred L. Standley and Louis H. Pratt (Jackson: University Press of Mississippi, 1989), 1-3.

38. Baldwin, "The Devil Finds Work," 481.

39. Baldwin, "The Discovery of What It Means to Be an American," in "Nobody Knows My Name," 138.

There's thousands of people
They ain't got no place to go.
My house fell down
And I can't live there no more.

Bessie sang the way Baldwin wanted to write. She faced the "disaster" of the Nashville flood, which nearly killed her, but she was not defeated. She went beyond it, telling the story of survival and triumph. He wanted to capture "her tone and her cadence" and express beauty in the tragedy, just like Bessie. She gave Baldwin back his experience, which is what black music does. When the blues artist gives black people back their experience, they can bear the suffering and embrace the joy and, with a little "imagination," take control of a "bad situation" and make the best of it. Blues artists, Baldwin wrote in a review of Stanley Dance's *The World of Earl Hines*, "have given more to the world than anyone can say. . . . They gave our sorrow and danger back to us, transformed, and they helped us to embrace and triumph over it. They gave back our joy and we could give it to our children. Out of the depths of the midnight hour, we could laugh."[40]

Not everyone would agree with what Baldwin says about the blues, but most blacks would. "It is only in his music," Baldwin writes, in "Many Thousand Gone," "that the Negro in America has been able to tell his story. . . . But it is not a very pretty story."[41] Yet it is our salvation during troubled times, our "rock in a weary land," and "shelter in the time of storm." "Yes," Baldwin continues in his reflection on the blues, "I,

---

40. Baldwin, "The Last of the Great Masters" (1977), in *Collected Essays*, 772.

41. Baldwin, "Many Thousands Gone," in "Notes of a Native Son," in *Collected Essays*, 19.

too, have said that I would exchange all the blues to save one starving child. I was wrong, not only because the exchange is not in my power, but because this singing of the Lord's song in so strange a land has saved more children than anyone will ever know, and the beginning is not yet in sight."[42]

In "The Devil Finds Work," Baldwin cites the well-known words of T. S. Eliot, "people cannot bear very much reality,"[43] and uses them to make his point about "the uses of the blues."[44] "In order for a person to bear his life, he needs a valid re-creation of that life, which is why, as Ray Charles might put it, blacks chose to sing the blues."[45] In an interview, Baldwin referred to the blues artist as a poet.

> Billie Holiday was a poet. She gave you back your experience. She refined it, you recognized it for the first time because she was in and out of it and she made it possible for you to bear it. And if you could bear it, then you could begin to change it. That's what a poet does. I'm not talking about books. I'm talking about a certain kind of passion, a certain kind of energy which people produce and they secrete in certain kind of people like Billie Holiday, Nina Simone, and Max Roach because they need it and these people give it back to you and they get you one place to another.[46]

Although I never met James Baldwin, I heard him speak in 1980 at McMillan Hall (now Miller Theater) of Columbia

---

42. Baldwin, "The Last of the Great Masters," 772.
43. Baldwin, "The Devil Finds Work," 524.
44. See Baldwin, "The Uses of the Blues," 57–66.
45. Baldwin, "The Devil Finds Work," 524.
46. "Black Scholar Interviews James Baldwin" (1973), in *Conversations,* 143.

University with Toni Morrison and Amiri Baraka, at a Forum on "Black Literature in the 80s: Revolution or Renaissance." He was even more impressive than I'd imagined. I could see that Morrison and Baraka deferred to him, as was appropriate, treating him with respect as a literary father. While Morrison and Baraka held their own, reading from their works with grace and power, I was there to hear Baldwin. He did not disappoint: "The price of becoming articulate in this country or in the West was to lie about your experience."[47] As he knew so well, the blues didn't lie; they told a brutal truth.

Ever since then, Baldwin joined my intellectual trinity along with Martin King and Malcolm X. They told the truth about black people, and that's why we still remember them. Baldwin shared Martin King's incredible *love* of humanity. And he shared his *rage*, defined by love of *blackness*, with Malcolm X. Malcolm, Baldwin said to Kenneth Clark, tells black people "they should be proud of being black, and God knows they should be. That is a very important thing to hear in a country which assures you that you should be ashamed of it."[48]

Nobody could preach love like Martin; nobody could talk black like Malcolm; and nobody could write with eloquence about love and blackness like Baldwin. When I want to know what it means to speak with power, I listen to recordings of Martin or Malcolm. They were artists of the spoken word. They could play an audience the way Louis Armstrong could play his trumpet. But when I want to know what it means to write with power, I turn to James Baldwin. His language

---

47. See an account of the event in C. Gerald Fraser, "Black Writers on Their Publishing Future," *New York Times*, November 27, 1980, C19.
48. Clark, *King, Malcolm, Baldwin*, 59.

reads as though a transcendent spirit inspired his words. God must write like that. I read his words like scripture.

Baldwin loved all human beings. "If you really love one person," he said, "you will love all people."[49] What angered him is that white America did not love black people and did not even treat them as human beings. Speaking to a white audience, Baldwin began his address with the shocking statement, "I am not a nigger," and people could feel his anger, reacting nervously to his use of the epithet "nigger." "I am a man!" he declared with great passion. "The question is, 'Why do you need a nigger?'" When he talked about the savage treatment of black people in the United States, he spoke with a rage, rather like Malcolm X; but he was not a separatist like Malcolm in the Nation of Islam. Instead, Baldwin, Martin King, other civil rights activists, and freedom fighters in Mecca and Africa influenced Malcolm to reject the separatist beliefs of the Nation of Islam and to become a passionate lover of humanity. Love is what gets people through suffering and through life whole and undefeated.

Martin, Malcolm, and Jimmy brought a different perspective, and those three defined my own. Recently, visiting Rahway State Prison in New Jersey and Sing Sing Prison in Ossining, New York, I was talking to inmates about how to bear their reality. Knowing that this is a tremendous challenge, I took Baldwin with me, speaking with his words: "If we are what our circumstances make us, we are, also, what we make of our circumstances."[50] The men in the audience smiled and nodded. Then I talked about Malcolm X, whose life and message they had read in his *Autobiography* and my

---

49. Cited in Leeming, *James Baldwin*, 125.
50. Baldwin, "Every Good-bye Ain't Gone," in *Collected Essays*, 776.

·

Martin & Malcolm & America. Since Malcolm was in Charlestown State Prison in Massachusetts for seven years, they connected with him: "Don't be shocked when I tell you I was in prison," he told a Detroit audience in one of his most famous talks, "Message to the Grass Roots" (November 1963). "You're still in prison. That's what America means: prison."[51] Five months later, in another well-known Detroit talk, "The Ballot or the Bullet" (April 1964), he used the prison image to challenge blacks to fight against the hypocrisy of American democracy. "If you go to jail, so what? If you are black, you are born in jail."[52] Inmates resonated with Malcolm's life and words, the same as blacks at the juke joint connected with blues artists. He gave inmates back their experience, transformed. With education and religion, they saw how Malcolm could bear his reality, which helped them bear theirs; for me, as for them, reading Malcolm and Baldwin was like listening to the blues.

When I read Baldwin, suffering became real. No abstract talk, just the plain truth blacks have lived. No writer could describe black suffering like Baldwin:

> This past, the Negro's past, of rope, fire, torture, castration, infanticide, rape; death and humiliation; fear by day and night, fear as deep as the marrow in the bone; doubt that he was worthy of life, since everyone around him denied it; sorrow for his women, for his kinfolk, for his children, who needed his protection, and whom he could not protect; rage, hatred, and murder, hatred for

---

51. *Malcolm X Speaks*, ed. George Breitman (New York: Grove Press, 1965), 8.

52. Malcolm X, "The Ballot or the Bullet," April 12, 1964, Detroit, MI. http://malcolmxfiles.blogspot.com.

white men so deep that it often turned against him and his own, and made all love, all trust, all joy impossible.[53]

There is hardly a black person alive who does not know in his flesh and bones what Baldwin is writing about. He gives us back our experience, and it makes us mad at what white people did to our grandparents and continue to do to us today. When I read that passage to my Baldwin class, black students, staring at the white students in their midst, found it difficult to restrain their anger and seemed ready to fight, while the white students, heads down, grew silent and ready to bolt the room. Then I continued reading from Baldwin where I left off, and black students turned their anger toward Baldwin. "This past, this endless struggle to achieve and reveal and confirm a human identity, human authority, yet contains, for all its horror, something very beautiful."

Hand went up! "Stop right there! Professor Cone," one black student interrupted me, "is Baldwin crazy? What the hell is beautiful about black suffering—slavery, segregation and lynching?"

"Hear him out," I replied. "You owe him that. He is your elder, perhaps 'the most important writer in the twentieth century,'[54] and has experienced much of the suffering he is describing."

I do not mean to be sentimental about suffering, [Baldwin writes] . . . but people who cannot suffer can never grow up, can never discover who they are. That man who is forced each day to snatch his manhood, his iden-

---

53. Baldwin, "The Fire Next Time," 342.
54. JoAnn Wypijewski, "A Guide in Dark Times: Why It's Essential to Read James Baldwin Now," *The Nation*, February 9, 2015, 4.

tity, out of the fire of human cruelty that rages to destroy it knows, if he survives his effort, and even if he does not survive it, something about himself and human life that no school on earth—and, indeed, no church—can teach. He achieves his own authority, and that is unshakeable. This is because, in order to save his life, he is forced to look beneath appearances, to take nothing for granted, to hear the meaning behind the words. If one is continually surviving the worst that life can bring, one eventually ceases to be controlled by fear of what life can bring; whatever it brings must be borne. And at this level of experience one's bitterness begins to be palatable, and hatred becomes too heavy a sack to carry.[55]

Most black students were not satisfied with what Baldwin writes about the beauty in black suffering. White students were silent. I understood their objections and silence. No rational black person can see beauty in a lynched victim or any other senseless mob brutality against black people. And whites should have a respectful silence about black anger. Don't ask for forgiveness and leave it at that. We have experienced too much legalized and vigilante violence.

But Baldwin is not being rational. He is *theological*, without calling it that. He may have left the pulpit, but he didn't stop preaching or interpreting. Hilton Als correctly says, "Baldwin could not distinguish between writing sermons and making art."[56] I'm glad he couldn't because that would have been like taking the "Come-to-Jesus Stuff" out of *Mountain*, which, to

---

55. Baldwin, "The Fire Next Time," 342–43.
56. Hilton Als, "The Enemy Within: The Making and Unmaking of James Baldwin," *The New Yorker*, February 16, 1998, 80.

Baldwin's horror, an editor had actually suggested.[57] The art in Baldwin is his preaching, and preaching is his art. They cannot be separated. They go together. That's not a weakness but a strength. In "Fire," he is being religious (read theological). He is probing deep down into the paradoxical dimension of the human spirit, what black preachers call the inscrutable and the mysterious—that part of human meaning no one can really explain but you know it's true. The truth is revealed in what one feels. This is the truth that makes us free. You know deep inside yourself that God created worth in all human beings that nobody can destroy no matter what they do.

What was beautiful about slavery? Nothing, rationally! But the spirituals, folklore, slave religion, and slave narratives *are* beautiful, and they came out of slavery. How do we explain that miracle? What's beautiful about lynching and Jim Crow segregation? Nothing! Yet the blues, jazz, great preaching, and gospel music *are* beautiful, and they came out of the post-slavery brutalities of white supremacy. In the 1960s we proclaimed "Black is beautiful!" because it is. We raised our fists to "I'm Black and I'm Proud," and we showed "Black Pride" in our walk and talk, our song and sermon.

We were not destroyed by white supremacy. We resisted it, created a beautiful culture, the civil rights and Black Power movements, which are celebrated around the world. Baldwin asked black people "to accept the past and to learn to live with it." "I beg the black people of this country," he

---

57. See James Baldwin, *The Amen Corner* (New York: Dial Press, 1968), xiv. See also Barbara K. Olson, "'Come-to-Jesus Stuff' in James Baldwin's *Go Tell It on the Mountain* and *The Amen Corner*," *African American Review* 31, no. 2 (Summer 1997): 295–301.

said, shortly after "Fire" was published, "to do something which I know to be very difficult; to be proud of the auction block, and all that rope, and all that fire, and all that pain."[58]

To see beauty in tragedy is very difficult. One needs theological eyes to do that. We have to look beneath the surface and get to the source. Baldwin was not blind. He saw both the tragedy and the beauty in black suffering and its redeeming value. That was why he said that suffering can become a *bridge* that connects people with one another, blacks with whites and people of all cultures with one another. Suffering is sorrow and joy, tragedy and triumph. It connected blacks with one another and made us stronger. We know anguish and pain and have moved beyond it. The real question about suffering is how to use it. "If you can accept the pain that almost kills you," says Vivaldo, Baldwin's character in his novel *Another Country*, "you can use it, you can become better." But "that's hard to do," Eric, another character, responds. "I know," Vivaldo acknowledges. If you don't accept the pain, "you get stopped with whatever it was that ruined you and you make it happen over and over again and your life has—ceased, really—because you can't move or change or love anymore."[59] But if you accept it, "you realize that your suffering does not isolate you," Baldwin says in his dialogue with Nikki Giovanni; "your suffering is your

---

58. See *Time*, May 17, 1963: "At the root of the Negro problem is the necessity of the white man to find a way of living with the Negro in order to live with himself." Baldwin is on the cover, even though there is a little longer story about Martin Luther King Jr. in Birmingham, entitled "Freedom—Now."

59. James Baldwin, "Another Country," in *Early Novels & Short Stories*, ed. Toni Morrison (New York: Library of America, 1998), 716.

bridge."[60] Singing the blues and the spirituals is using suffering, letting it become your bridge moving forward. "For, while the tale of how we suffer, and how we are delighted, and how we may triumph is never new, it always must be heard," Baldwin writes in his short story "Sonny's Blues." "There isn't any other tale to tell, and it's the only light we've got in all this darkness."[61]

People bleed when they are beaten, shot, and castrated. They hurt in body, mind, and soul. But as Baldwin emphasizes, everybody suffers. Death is universal, an equalizer. One day, death will knock on everybody's door, always uninvited—both for the rich and the poor, old and young, black and white, male and female. No one escapes. Slaves created songs about death.

> Soon one mornin', death comes a-creepin' in my room,
> Oh my Lawd, Oh my Lawd, what shall I do?

> Death done been here, tuck my mother an' gone,
> Oh my Lawd, what shall I do?

"There is no way not to suffer," Baldwin writes. "Everybody born . . . until the whole thing is over, is certain of one thing: he is going to suffer."[62]

We can also be certain that everyone pays for what they do to others and to themselves. Not everybody uses suffer-

---

60. James Baldwin and Nikki Giovanni, *Baldwin and Giovanni: A Dialogue* (Philadelphia: Lippincott, 1973), 74.

61. Baldwin, "Sonny's Blues," in "Going to Meet the Man," in *Early Novels & Stories*, ed. Toni Morrison (New York: Library of America, 1998), 862. This quotation was cited on Baldwin's funeral program.

62. Baldwin, "The Uses of the Blues," in "Go Tell It on the Mountain," in *Early Novels & Stories*, 59.

ing as a bridge. Suffering also separates people when they
don't recognize one another as human beings. If you don't
regard another person as human like you, his or her suffering will not faze you. When we fail to acknowledge another's
humanity, we pay for our blindness. It is easy for the poor to
think that the rich get by without paying anything for what
they do, but that's not the case. "People pay for what they
do, and, still more," Baldwin writes, "for what they have
allowed themselves to become. And they pay for it very simply: by the lives they lead"—wasted lives, empty lives, mean-
ingless lives. Who would want to be shaped by a family that
lynched people, or by a culture and religion that accepted
slavery, segregation, and white supremacy? Children have
to be taught to hate. I have seen white people shaped by a
culture of racial hatred. It is not a pretty sight.

In my television dialogue with Bill Moyers I told him flat-
out that I would rather be a part of the culture that resisted
lynching than the one that lynched. I would rather be the one
who suffered wrong than the one who did wrong. The one
who suffered wrong is stronger than the one who did wrong.
Jesus was stronger than his crucifiers. Blacks are stronger
than whites. Black religion is more creative and meaningful
and true than white religion. That is why I love black religion, folklore, and the blues. Black culture keeps black people
from hating white people. Every Sunday morning, we went
to church to exorcize hate—of ourselves and of white racists.
That's what the preaching, shouting, praying, and singing
were about. No one could describe it better than Baldwin:

> There is no music like that music, no drama like the
> drama of the saints rejoicing, the sinners moaning,

the tambourines racing, and all those voices coming together and crying holy unto the Lord. There is still, for me, no pathos quite like the pathos of those multicolored, worn, somehow triumphant and transfigured faces, speaking for a depth of a visible, tangible, continuing despair of the goodness of the Lord. I have never seen anything to equal the fire and excitement that sometimes, without warning, fill a church, causing the church, as Leadbelly and so many others have testified, to "rock." Nothing that has happened to me since equals the power and the glory that I sometimes felt when, in the middle of a sermon, I knew that I was somehow, by some miracle, really carrying, as they said, "the Word"—when the church and I were one. Their pain and their joy were mine and, and mine were theirs—they surrendered their pain and joy to me, I surrendered mine to them—and their cries of "Amen!" and "Hallelujah!" and "Yes, Lord!" and "Praise His name!" and "Preach it, brother!" sustained and whipped on my solos until we all became equal, wringing wet, singing and dancing, in anguish and rejoicing, at the foot of the altar.[63]

Black religion and culture got black people through difficult times, through a "trouble in mind."

Darryl Pinckney correctly calls Baldwin "the apostle of paradox."[64] There is something deeply paradoxical and

---

63. Baldwin, "The Fire Next Time," 306.

64. Darryl Pinckney, "The Magic of James Baldwin," *The New York Review of Books*, November 19, 1998, 70.

truthful in what Baldwin says about suffering. His message is hard to accept, and he knows it. He states one truth that is acceptable and another that is not. But through reading Baldwin, I realized that if I were going to understand anything about suffering, rational thinking was not enough. I had to learn suffering from the people who have suffered and overcome.

Conclusion

As I come to the end of my theological journey, I can't stop thinking about black blood: the blood of Denise McNair (age 11), Carole Robertson, Cynthia Wesley, and Addie Mae Collins (14)—four black girls in Birmingham, Alabama; Emmett Till (14), Trayvon Martin, Jordan Davis (17), and Michael Brown (18)—four teenage black boys from the North and South. These children, whose names should never be forgotten, were lynched by white men and became symbols of the horrific violence of white supremacy in our time. Whether fifty years ago or today, white men seem to think that they have the right to murder black people, knowing that no jury or judge will convict them for killing niggers. Black lives don't matter to them. Never have.

Cain killed his brother, Abel. But Abel's blood spoke: "Then the Lord said to Cain, 'Where is your brother Abel?' He said, 'I don't know; am I my brother's keeper?' And the Lord said, 'What have you done? Listen: your brother's blood is crying out to me from the ground!'" (Gen 4:9-10)

Cain can be viewed as a metaphor for white people and Abel for black people. God is asking white Americans, especially Christians, "Where are your black brothers and sisters?" And whites respond, "We don't know. Are we their keepers?" And the Lord says, "What have you done to them for four centuries?"

The blood of black people is crying out to God and to white people from the ground in the United States of America. The blood of Sandra Bland in Texas and Tamir Rice in Ohio; the blood of the Emanuel Nine in Charleston, South Carolina, and Eric Garner in Staten Island, New York; the blood of nearly five thousand lynched blacks; and the blood of Nat Turner, Denmark Vesey, and Gabriel Prosser, and the "many thousands gone," millions gone on the auction block, under the lash, and during the Middle Passage. Black blood is crying out to God all over this land. Is anybody listening to the cries of black blood, that "strange fruit" that Billie Holiday sang about, "blood on the leaves and blood at the root"?

The cry of black blood that I heard in Detroit (1967) more than fifty years ago is still crying out all over America today. White people didn't hear it then, and they still don't hear it now. They are deaf to the cry of black blood. Yet black people will not be silent as our children are thrown in rivers, blown into eternity, and shot dead in the streets. Black Lives Matter! God hears that cry, and black liberation theology bears witness to it.

There is no future for America without black people. The identity of America and black people is inextricably bound together. There is nothing white people can do to separate us from this land. "The land is ours because we come out of it, our tears watered it, we fertilized it with our dead," proclaimed Reverend Hickman, a character in Ralph Ellison's novel *Juneteenth*. "The more of us they destroy the more it becomes filled with the spirit of our redemption."[1] But they

---

1. See an excerpt of Ellison's novel in *Living with Music: Ralph Ellison's Jazz Writings*, ed. and intro. Robert G. O'Mealy (New York: Modern Library, 2001), 210–11.

can't kill all of us and they can't put all of us in jails and prisons. Whites must treat blacks as human beings or they will never have peace and tranquility in this land. Black people are the disturbers of the peace in America. We are the troublemakers. When whites speak of freedom, justice, and equality, we ask: What freedom? What justice? What equality? Whites cannot look blacks in the eye and talk about freedom, justice, and equality without shame and hypocrisy.

"The white man prefers to keep the black man at a certain human remove because it is easier for him . . . to . . . avoid being called to account for the crimes committed by his forefathers, or his neighbors."[2] That is why so many whites live in segregated, gated communities. They cannot bear to see blacks every day because we remind them of the lies they tell themselves and the world. We are their conscience. As Martin Luther King Jr. did, so also black liberation theology tries to prick the conscience of white people, even when it often seems, as Malcolm X said, that they have no conscience.

Black people are resilient. We will never stop fighting for our humanity. I write because writing is the way I fight. Teaching is the way I resist, doing what I can to subvert white supremacy. We will wear down whites with our resistance and determination to be free. And we *will* be free. Once people resist, they never stop. Resistance births hope. Hope pushes people forward and makes them believe nothing is impossible. As King said, we must learn to live

---

2. James Baldwin, "Stranger in the Village," in *Collected Essays*, ed. Toni Morrison (New York: Library of America, 1998), 122.

together as human beings, treating one another with dignity and respect, or we will perish together as fools. There is no other choice. I choose life.

We can't live together with whites without being *black*. We can't respect whites without first respecting ourselves. Martin King knew that, but he didn't say it enough, thus allowing white people, and some black people too, to underestimate his challenge. That was why we needed Malcolm X to remind us that we are black *first* and everything else second. White people don't like talking about Malcolm X because his fierce affirmation of blackness frightens them. But blackness is a part of the DNA of black people. We cannot be human without being black, and we cannot live with whites without being human.

James Baldwin was with me when I began writing black liberation theology, and he will be with me when I stop. Baldwin is like a two-edged sword. He cuts both ways: Martin and Malcolm, love and blackness, whites and blacks and others too. America is a "Beloved Community" in the making, a human family, with all kinds of people in it— different races and sexual orientations, different sizes and shapes, both able and differently able, and a whole lot of other things. James Baldwin has emerged as a prophet in our time because he embodied in his life and art our great diversity and embraced it with joy.

A British interviewer once asked him: "When you started out as a writer, you were black, impoverished, homosexual, you must have said to yourself, 'Gee, how disadvantaged can I get?'" "No, I thought I hit the jackpot!" Baldwin replied with his radiant smile, his audience bursting into laughter, as he embraced the moment to identify with human diversity, especially the marginalized part many people reject.

America has hit the jackpot and doesn't even know it. But we, like Baldwin, need to embrace our diversity with joy, knowing that we are stronger and better as a nation when we embrace the weak—the least in our midst. That's what makes me proud to be an American—an *African* American. What a blessing!

Acknowledgments

This book would not be possible without the assistance of many people. Nkosi Anderson, my research assistant, was invaluable, finding newspaper articles and books in libraries. He also assisted me in my classes, enabling me to focus on teaching and writing.

Jamall Calloway was also helpful, reading the entire manuscript and offering helpful suggestions.

I also want to thank all the students of more than fifty years at Philander Smith (Little Rock, Arkansas) and Adrian (Michigan) Colleges and at Union Theological Seminary.

Union students, faculty, administration, staff, and board of directors deserve a special thanks for their enormous support of my ministry of teaching and scholarship.

Victoria Furio, my administrative assistant of eighteen years, also deserves special thanks. Without her capacity to efficiently handle the great volume of detail involved in supporting my teaching and lecturing, and protecting me from everyone, except my students and colleagues, who wanted to talk to me about black liberation theology, I would not have been able to write and teach effectively. She also was the first to read my manuscript and offered encouragement and critique.

I don't have words to express adequately my gratitude to all my doctoral students (more than forty) who supported and challenged me and then moved beyond me. I am appreciative of black scholars (women and men) in all disciplines who have developed black theology and religion into a major voice in the academy and the church. I hope they can see the contributions they have made in my reflections on black liberation theology.

I want to express my deepest thanks to my colleague and close friend, Elaine Pagels, who has participated in the process of this writing every step of the way.

Robert Ellsberg, my editor at Orbis for many years, was encouraging from the moment I told him about the possibility of writing this book. His expert editorial hand has been invaluable, protecting me from myself, cutting the clutter, so my voice comes through as clearly and powerfully as possible. But most of all, I am deeply grateful for his friendship.

I want to thank my son Charles for reading and discussing my manuscript, always offering encouraging words, which I needed. He was writing his first fiction novel at the same time, which I read trying to do for him what he did for me, and our mutual reading deepened our love and bond of friendship. His mother and my ex-wife, Rose, is also much appreciated for reading the chapters that cover the time we were together and helped me to remember things about Garrett, Philander Smith, Adrian, and Union and my struggles with writing, and white people I had forgotten. I must mention my appreciation to my daughters, Krystal and Robynn, and my granddaughter, Jolie Henderson, and my son Michael and daughter-in-law, Janie, and grandson, Miles, for showering me with love and encouragement during my writing.

Lastly, I want to thank my devoted readers who have supported me more than a half century. To write books that people actually read is a thrilling and rewarding experience.

Index

Abelard, Peter, 122
absolutism, 112
Abu-Jamal, Mumia, on James
    Baldwin, 146
Achebe, Chinua, 124, 150
    on art and oppression, 64
Adams, James Luther, 74
Adrian College, 1, 2, 3, 6, 39, 40,
    62, 65, 70
African Methodist Episcopal
    Church, founding of, 41
Alexander, Michelle, on prison
    industrial complex, 136
Allen, Richard, 41
Als, Hilton, 163
anger, as beginning of theology,
    109
Anselm, 114, 122
Aristotle, 27
Arius, 27
Armstrong, Louis, 159
Athanasius, 27, 49, 109
Augustine, 27, 49, 112, 113, 114
Autobiography of Malcolm X, 13,
    114, 147, 149, 160

Baldwin, James, 1, 7, 13, 32, 74,
    116, 128
    on black religion and culture,
        167, 168
    on black self-hate, 60, 61, 92,
        141

    on black suffering, 161–69
    and the blues, 156–58, 164–
        166
    dialogue with Reinhold
        Niebuhr, 136
    disaffection with the church,
        145, 146, 155
    on embracing blackness, 91,
        92, 173, 174
    on God and Jesus, 16, 153,
        154, 155
    on God's love, 144
    on hatred, 138, 139
    influence of, 150, 151
    influence on James Cone, 127,
        137, 144–69, 173, 174
    letter to nephew, 153
    on love, 40, 113
    as lover of humanity, 160
    on lynching, 134
    as preacher, 145, 151, 163,
        164
    as prophet, 147, 148, 173
    on race relations, 57, 147
    on Richard Nixon, 153
    on suffering, 111, 152, 153
    as writer, 1, 21, 28, 29, 35, 64,
        83, 124, 125
    on writing from one's
        experience, 17, 30, 110
Baraka, Amiri. *See* Jones, LeRoi
Barmen Declaration, 10

Barth, Karl, 1, 2, 10, 11, 17, 27, 41,
    49, 62, 79, 80, 109, 112
    and black liberation theology,
        68
    Church Dogmatics, 58
    on God-talk, 122
Bartlett, Gene, 49
Beach, Waldo, 78, 79
Bennett, John, 51–54, 70, 72, 116
    on black theology as a fad,
        116
Bertocci, Peter A., 26
Bethel (independent African
    church), 41
"Beyond Vietnam" (address of
    Martin Luther King Jr.), 3
Black Christ, 46, 47, 79, 92, 98,
    118
    and Black Panthers, 103
black Christianity, as liberating,
    91
black church
    and black self-worth, 94
    lack of concern for training
        theologians, 59
    preaching in, 9
    and rise of civil rights
        movement, 42
black freedom, in spirituals and
    the blues, 95–98
black freedom movement, 32
black is beautiful, 98, 164, 165
black liberation theology, 171
    and black self-worth, 94
    origins of, 64
    and white European theolo-
        gians, 62, 63
    See also black theology
Black Lives Matter, 139, 143, 171
Black Messiah, 64
Black Methodists for Church
    Renewal (BMCR), 18

black music, 35
    and black freedom, 95–98
    and black liberation theology,
        64, 65, 92, 93, 94, 95–98
    and black systematic
        theology, 63
    as weapon of resistance, 138
The Black Muslims in America
    (C. Eric Lincoln), 19
black nationalism, 20, 61, 103,
    104, 105
Black Panthers, 77, 103, 104, 105
"The Black Paper," 18
Black Power, 12, 17, 98, 164
    and black theology, 21, 31–50
    condemnation of, 7, 10
    critique of, 90
    and the gospel, 9, 11, 12, 14,
        32, 36
    meaning of, 7, 8, 10, 13, 14, 18,
        19
    proclamation of, by Stokely
        Carmichael, 2, 12, 19
    and violence, 49
black racism, 57
black resistance, 164, 172, 173
    redemptive significance of,
        131, 132
Black Spirit, 43, 45, 47, 65, 139
black suffering, 124, 125, 138
    and black theology, 46, 93
    and Christian gospel, 129
black theology, 33, 41, 48
    African spirit of, 79
    and Black Christ, 79
    and the black experience, 88,
        89
    as black liberation, 75
    critique by black women, 119,
        120
    foundations of, 60
    and liberation, 65, 66, 71

and Marxism, 118, 119
national audience for, 77
secular sources of, 103
suffering as starting point, 46
as tribal theology, 78
and universalism of gospel,
49
and white theologians, 75, 76,
80, 81, 82
Black Theology and Black Power
(Cone), 35, 37, 48, 51, 52,
56, 60, 61, 70, 71, 74, 77, 86,
87, 88, 98, 103, 104, 149
as "Little Red Book," 72
theological topics and
perspectives in, 45, 46
A Black Theology of Liberation
(Cone), 61, 62, 63, 65, 67,
69, 77, 82, 85, 88
black theology students,
mentoring of, 116, 117
blackness, 7, 8, 12–17, 19, 22, 32,
42, 46, 61, 62
beauty of, 98, 141, 142, 164, 165
and liberation, 60, 61
and theology, 32, 33
blacks, and self-respect, 173
Bland, Bobby "Blue," 35
Bland, Sandra, 171
blues, 105, 106, 149, 166
as secular spirituals, 105, 106
Boff, Leonardo, 115
Bonhoeffer, Dietrich, 73, 135
and black liberation theology,
68
Boston University, 26
Boyack, James and Alice, 25, 26
Briggs, Charles A., 73
Brightman, Edgar S., 26
Brown, James, 13, 93
Brown, Michael, 170
Brunner, Emile, 10

and black liberation theology,
68
Buckley, Arthur, 48
Bultmann, Rudolph, 27, 62
and black liberation theology,
68

Calvin, John, 27, 49, 112
Camus, Albert, 13, 17, 124
Cannon, Katie, and social ethics,
120
Carmichael, Stokely
and black self-determination,
13
on empowering blacks, 47
and politics of liberation, 69
proclamation of Black Power,
2, 7, 9, 12, 19, 32, 48
Castile, Philando, 137
Charles, Ray, 92, 158
Charlestown State Prison, and
Malcolm X, 161
cheap grace, 135
Christ
identification with recrucified
black bodies, 133
lynching of, 128
See also Black Christ
Christian, and black, 60
Christianity
as religion of liberation, 83
as white man's religion, 60
"Christianity and Black Power"
(Cone lecture/essay), 11,
17, 29, 30, 48, 56, 74
civil rights movement, 15, 164
and lynching of Emmett Till,
131
and Martin Luther King, Jr.,
1, 15, 32, 40, 60, 69, 87
Clark, Kenneth, 152, 159
Cleage, Albert, 9, 14, 98, 104

Clement of Alexandria, 27
Colgate Rochester Divinity
    School, 31, 32, 48
Collins, Addie Mae, 170
Columbia University, 12, 13
Comstock, Gary, 108
Cone, James H.
    appointment to Union Theo-
        logical Seminary, 70–73
    aspiration to college teaching,
        38
    attitude toward white and
        black critics, 93
    and call to ministry, 37, 38
    critique of, by Charles Long,
        87–91
    and development of black
        theology, 42, 43, 44
    education of, 23–27
    encounter with Charles Long,
        43, 44
    as Father of Black Liberation
        Theology, 107, 116
    influence of James Baldwin
        on, 144–69
    misunderstood by colleagues,
        40
    as teacher of black history, 76,
        77
    and teaching theology at
        Union, 108–25
    as writer, 28, 29, 30, 35, 36, 39,
        40, 43, 132
    on writing to empower
        blacks, 47
Cone, Cecil (brother), 5, 22, 23,
    35, 97
Cone, Charles (brother), 23, 97
Cone, Charlie (father), 22, 57, 58,
    77, 78, 96, 97, 138, 141
Cone, Lucy (mother), 22, 57, 58,
    78, 96, 97, 138, 141, 142

Cone, Rose (wife), 33, 70, 77
Congress of African Peoples, 104
Counts, Dorothy, 1
cross
    in Christian tradition, 121–23,
        125, 131, 132, 139–41
    as decorative object, 140
    as instrument of terror, 133,
        134
    and lynching tree, 130, 131,
        132, 133, 134, 139, 140, 141
    as transcendent transvalua-
        tion of values, 123
The Cross and the Lynching Tree
    (Cone), 125, 126–43
crucifixion, meaning for blacks,
    128, 133, 139, 140
Cullen, Countee, 128, 129

Dance, Stanley, 157
Davis, Jordan, 170
Deloria, Vine, 88, 115
Descartes, René, 25
Detroit rebellion, 1, 2, 6, 7, 9, 147,
    148, 149, 150, 171
Donatists, 27
Dostoevsky, Fyodor, 124
Douglas, Kelly Brown, and
    womanist theology, 120
Du Bois, W. E. B., 61
Duke University Divinity School,
    78, 79
Dunbar, Paul Laurence, 3

Ecumenical Association of
    Third World Theologians
    (EATWOT), 115
Edward Waters College, 23
Eliade, Mircea, 43, 114
Ellacuría, Ignacio, and crucified
    peoples of history, 132
Ellison, Ralph, 171

Elmhurst College, 11, 17, 32
Emanuel Nine, 138, 139, 171
"The Ethics of Living Jim Crow"
(Richard Wright), 4
exodus
at center of black religion, 125
as liberation event in black
theology, 66, 67, 68, 81
experience, as beginning of
theology, 112

Fanon, Franz, 13
"The Fire Next Time" (Baldwin),
146, 147
Forbes, James, 118
forgiveness, and black
community, 138, 139
Frankl, Victor, 124
Franklin, Aretha, 13, 35, 93
Fund for Theological Education,
86

Garner, Eric, 171
Garnet, Henry Highland, address
to slaves, 41, 42
Garrett Theological Seminary, 2,
4, 6, 10, 16, 26, 27, 28, 36,
38, 79, 82, 99
Garrett-Evangelical. *See* Garrett
Theological Seminary
Garvey, Marcus, 61
Gaye, Marvin, 144
Gebara, Ivone, 124
Gibson, Kenneth, 103
Giovanni, Nikki, 14, 165
Go Tell It on the Mountain
(Baldwin), 28, 145, 154, 155,
156, 163
God of the Oppressed (Cone), 102,
103
Goetz, Ronald, 10, 11, 17
Goldwater, Barry, 3

Gospel Angelic Singers, 153
gospel of Jesus
and Black Power 9, 11, 12, 14,
32, 36, 71
and reality of black suffering,
60
Grant, Jacquelyn
on Jesus as a black woman,
110
and womanist theology, 120
Gutiérrez, Gustavo, 115, 124
and theology as response to
struggle for justice, 111

Hamer, Fannie Lou, 131, 137
Hamilton, Charles V., 12
Harlem Globetrotters, 142
Harnack, A. von, 10
Harris Franklin Roll Lectures, 82
Harrison, Beverly, 108
hatred, and black community,
131, 138, 139
Haynes, Marques, 142
Hegel, Georg Wilhelm Friedrich,
25
Heidegger, Martin, 27
Herzog, Fred, support for black
theology, 79
Heyward, Carter, 108
High John the Conqueror, 103,
155
history, and black liberation
theology, 77
Hitler, Adolf, 142
Holiday, Billie, 129, 134, 158
homophobia, 108, 110
Hordern, William E., 27, 28, 38,
39, 79
Howard University, 74
Hume, David, 25
Hunter, Reverend, 96
Hurt, John, 153

imagination, and theology, 91, 122

Ingersoll Lecture (Harvard University), 127

integrationists, 20, 21

Interdenominational Theological Center (Atlanta), 75

Is God a White Racist? (William Jones), 90

Jackson, Mahalia, 35, 95

Jackson, Samuel L., 151

Jenna Six, 130

Jeremias, Joachim, 27

Jesus of Nazareth
    as black woman, 110
    as criminal Jew, 145, 146
    as gay, 110
    prophetic and apocalyptic language of, 114
    as slave, 80
    as theme of black theology, 67

Jim Crow segregation, 37, 42, 62, 79, 91, 142

Jones, Absalom, 41

Jones, Lawrence N., 73

Jones, LeRoi (Amiri Baraka), 13, 45, 103, 104, 159
    on James Baldwin, 146

Jones, William, 90, 91, 102

justice, struggle for, 13, 14, 16, 47, 60, 87, 95
    and theology, 111, 117

Kafka, Franz, 143

Kant, Immanuel, 25

Karenga, Maulana, 46

Käsemann, Ernst, 27

Kierkegaard, Søren, 10

King, B. B., 35, 92, 95, 142

King, Martin Luther, Jr., 20, 26, 38, 145, 172
    assassination of, 33, 34, 35
    on Black Power, 7
    and black self-respect, 173
    and black suffering, 125
    on blacks and Vietnam War, 3, 137
    as civil right leader, 1, 15, 32, 40, 60, 69, 87
    experience in black church, 57
    influence on Cone, 99, 142, 149, 159
    on interrelatedness of life, 111
    on love and forgiveness, 139
    on loving one's enemy, 113
    and nonviolence, 12, 78, 113, 139
    rejection of separatism, 160
    and struggle for justice, 60, 137

Kirby, Miss, 24

Kitagawa, Joseph, 43

Lee, Don, 13, 14

Lehmann, Paul, 18, 70, 71
    support for black theology, 79, 80

liberation
    and black theology, 65, 66
    and blackness, 60, 61
    as central message of Bible, 81
    and civil rights movement, 68, 69
    and freedom, in black liberation theology, 69
    at heart of Christian theology, 66, 67
    as problematic theme in theology, 121

liberation theology, Latin American, 115. *See also* black liberation theology

life, interrelatedness of, 111
Lincoln, C. Eric, 32, 50, 65
    and Cone's appointment
        at Union Theological
        Seminary, 54, 55
    influence on Cone, 19, 20, 31,
        44, 67, 74, 76, 77, 99, 100,
        101, 102, 107
"Little Red Book," 72
Long, Charles H., 43, 44, 65, 86,
    107
    critique of black theology, 85,
        86, 87, 102
    critique of Cone's writings,
        87, 88, 89, 91
    on freedom from oppression,
        95
Louis, Joe, 141
love, as a battle, 113
Luther, Martin, 17, 27, 49, 109
lynched black bodies, as symbols
    of Christ's body, 140
lynching, 26, 37, 42, 49, 71, 79, 91,
    125, 170, 171
    of blacks and of Christ, 128,
        129, 130, 131
    twenty-first-century, 137
lynching tree
    as America's cross, 128, 129,
        139, 140, 141
    and black suffering, 127
    as a cross, 80
    as instrument of terror, 133,
        134

Macedonia AME Church (in
    Bearden), 24
Malcolm X, 31, 40, 113, 137, 146
    as Black Power advocate, 12,
        32, 49, 60, 71, 87, 125, 173
    and black self-hate, 92

    and black self-respect, 173
    on Christianity as white
        man's religion, 60
    criticism of, 57
    improvisional militant style
        of, 63
    influence on black liberation
        theology, 125
    influence on Cone, 7, 8, 13, 20,
        103, 149, 159
    and search for meaning, 114
    as separatist, 160
    spirit of blackness of, 62
    on treatment of blacks by
        whites, 34, 71
Martin & Malcolm & America
    (Cone), 124, 125
Martin, Trayvon, 170
Marty, Martin E., on Merton and
    Baldwin, 148
Mays, Benjamin E., 38, 39, 99,
    100, 101, 107
    review of *The Spirituals and
        the Blues*, 100
Mays, Willie, 142
McKay, Claude, 30
McKinney, Mildred W., 24
McNair, Denise, 170
McQuarrie, John, 70
Mead, Margaret, 145, 146, 151,
    152
Meeropol, Abel, 129
Meredith March, 19
Merton, Thomas, on James
    Baldwin, 148
Moltmann, Jürgen, on crucifixion
    of Jesus, 122
Moral Man and Immoral Society
    (Reinhold Niebuhr), 52
Morehouse College, 38
Morris Brown College, 38

Morrison, Toni, 124, 127, 137, 159
Moyers, Bill, 130, 131, 167

Nation of Islam, 12, 61, 160
National Committee of Black
    Churchmen, 19
National Committee of Negro
    Churchmen. *See* National
    Committee of Black
    Churchmen
National Conference of Black
    Churches (NCBC)
    promotion of black power and
        black theology, 117, 118
    statement on black theology,
        75, 98
National Football League players,
    protest of black killings, 139
Native Son (Richard Wright), 28
Nicholson, J. W., 38
Niebuhr, H. Richard, 73
Niebuhr, Reinhold, 27, 41, 49, 51,
    52, 55, 73, 74, 119
    and black liberation theology,
        68
    blindness to black oppression,
        135, 136
    critique of liberalism, 52
    on the cross, 123
    and practice of theology, 112
    review of *Black Theology and
        Black Power*, 52, 53
    on ultimate reality and
        imagination, 91
Nietzsche, Friedrich, 27
Nixon, Richard, 153
Northwestern University, 2, 4,
    27, 36

Obama, Barack, 131
Origen, 27

Owens, Jesse, 141, 142

Paul, Nathaniel, on God's
    passivity before slavery, 42
Payne, Daniel A., on existence of
    God, 42
Peck, Raoul, 151
Philander Smith College, 25, 27,
    38, 39, 62, 70
Pickett, Wilson, 106
Pinckney, Darryl, 168
Plato, 27, 114
Plotinus, 114
preaching, and systematic theol-
    ogy, 59
Prince (musician), 62
prison, America as, 161
prison industrial complex, and
    New Jim Crow, 136
prophets
    and black experience, 66
    and justice, 81
    killing of, 113
    and liberation, in black
        theology, 67, 68
    proclamation of liberation, 15
    solidarity with the poor, 114
Prosser, Gabriel, 171

racism, 3, 27, 34, 40, 57, 74, 115
    support by white theologians,
        58, 59
    in white churches, 61
Rahway State Prison, Cone's talk
    with inmates, 160, 161
Randall, Dudley, 14
Rauschenbusch, Walter, 31
"Recrucified Christ" (Countee
    Cullen), 128
redemptive suffering, womanist
    critique of, 127

Rice, Tamir, 171
Riley, Negail, 19, 20
riots (1960s), 147, 148, 149
Ritschl, Albrecht, 10
Riverside Church (New York
      City), 3, 118
Roach, Max, 158
Roberts, J. Deotis, 74, 75
      critique of Cone's work, 90,
      91, 102
Roberts, Samuel K., 118
Robertson, Carole, 170
Robinson, Jackie, 142
Roof, Dylan, 138, 139
Rooks, Charles Shelby, 86

Saint John the Divine Cathedral
      Church, Cone lecture on
      Baldwin at, 150
Sanchez, Sonia, 14
Scherer, Lester B., 9, 29, 30, 44, 70
Schleiermacher, Friedrich, 10
Schmeling, Max, 141
Scott, Walter, 137
self-hate, black, 8, 92, 61, 106
self-interrogation, 105
Shinn, Roger, 70
Shorter (Junior College), 25
Shrine of the Black Madonna
      (Detroit), 14
Simone, Nina, 50, 158
Sing Sing Prison, Cone's talk
      with inmates, 160, 161
Sisters in the Wilderness (Delores
      Williams), 121
Sixteenth Street Baptist Church
      (Birmingham, AL),
      bombing of, 136
slavery, 24, 29, 37, 41, 42, 69, 71,
      72, 78, 79, 91, 107, 133, 135,
      138, 142, 164, 167
Smith, Bessie, 156, 157

Society for the Study of Black
      Religion, 44, 85, 86
Soelle, Dorothee, 124
spirituals, 95–98
      and blues, 105, 106
The Spirituals and the Blues
      (Cone), 88, 95, 97, 102
St. George Methodist Episcopal
      Church (Philadelphia), 41
Sterling, Alton, 137
Stevens, Wallace, on God and
      imagination, 91
Stonewall Rebellion, 108, 110
"Strange Fruit" (Abel Meeropol),
      129, 134
suffering, as theological problem,
      123, 124, 125
Systematic Theology (Paul Tillich),
      58
systematic theology, for black
      people, 58, 59

Tatum, Goose, 142
teaching, connection with love,
      112, 113
Terkel, Studs, 92
theodicy, 90, 91
theology
      Christian, as black theology,
          60, 83
      and imagination, 91, 122
      and preaching, 59
      See also black theology; black
          liberation theology
A Theology of Liberation
      (Gutiérrez), 115
Thomas Aquinas, 112
Thurman, Howard, 98, 99, 100,
      107
      on Cone's work of black
          liberation theology, 99–101
      as prophetic mystic, 31

Till, Emmett, 26, 131, 170
Tillich, Paul, 1, 27, 41, 49, 55, 62,
     73, 74
  and black liberation theology,
     68
Turner, Henry McNeal, on God
     as a Negro, 42
Turner, Nat, 171
12th Street Riot, 1. *See also* Detroit
     rebellion

Union Presbyterian Seminary, 118
Union Theological Seminary
     (New York), 18, 51, 70–73,
     109, 112, 116
  as birthplace of black libera-
     tion and womanist theol-
     ogy, 117, 118
  black faculty at, 118
Union Theological Seminary
     (Richmond, VA), 118
University of the Pacific, 76

Vesey, Denmark, 171
Vietnam War, 2, 3, 34, 137, 144

Wallace, Sister Ora, 142
Washington, James, 118
Waters, Muddy, 92, 142
Watson, Philip S., 5, 6, 28, 56, 57,
     82, 83, 84, 108
Weatherby, W. J., on James
     Baldwin, 146
Wells, Ida B., 137
Wesley, Cynthia, 170
Wesley, John, 27
West, Cornel, 118, 119
white Christ, 64, 118
white Christianity, and lynching,
     135
white church, as Antichrist, 51,
     53, 54

white Jesus, 61
white supremacy, 8, 9, 11, 18, 22,
     30, 36, 37, 46, 47, 48, 49, 59,
     92, 105, 139, 172, 173
  as America's original sin, 54
  ignored by white theologians,
     74
  liberating Christians from, 61
  rejection of religion of, 64
white theologians
  and black liberation, 74
  and black theology, 75, 76, 78,
     79, 80, 81, 82
  blindness to black oppression,
     135
  and gospel of liberation, 71
  and ignorance of white
     supremacy, 74
white theology, 9, 15
  and seminary education, 61,
     62
  racism in, 22, 57, 64, 71, 94
  as tribal theology, 78
whites, and becoming black, 47
Williams, Daniel Day, 70
Williams, Delores
  critique of redemptive
     suffering, 121, 122, 123
  and womanist theology, 119,
     120, 121, 124, 125
Williams, Rowan, and self-
     interrogation, 105
Wilmore, Gayraud, 93
  as critic of Cone, 47, 48, 90, 91,
     102
womanist theology, critique of
     redemptive suffering, 127
Wright, Richard, 4, 13, 28, 29,
     127, 137
writing, as form of prayer, 143